Restoration Millionaire

A Guide to Building and Scaling a Restoration Empire

Alex Duta

STONE CREST
www.stonecrestbooks.com

STONE CREST BOOKS
www.StoneCrestBooks.com

First Edition
Published in the United States by Stone Crest Books
Stone Crest Books | www.StoneCrestBooks.com

For more information, visit RestorationMillionaire.com

ISBN: 978-1-961462-11-3 (hardcover)
978-1-961462-10-6 (paperback)
978-1-961462-09-0 (ebook)
978-1-961462-12-0 (audiobook)

PRAISE FOR RESTORATION MILLIONAIRE

"I've always been drawn to those who go through life as an "open book". Everyone is more than happy to discuss their best traits and stories, few have the guts to reveal their warts for the world to see. Alex and I met two years ago when he was a finalist for the R&R Ladder Award, and I was a newcomer to the industry. A young, confident man, it was easy to see how he became successful. But pull some of the layers of the Onion away, as he does in this great book, and you will learn about the scars he acquired and the difficulties he went through to reach the success he has. "Restoration Millionaire" is an honest, thoughtful, and very timely piece designed to provide a roadmap to success for both those entering the Restoration industry, as well as established veterans. Avoid the "Reactive Rollercoaster", brush off the disappointments that will surely come, and follow the trail discussed by Alex in this book. You won't regret it!"

—Michael Balzano, Publisher, Restoration & Remediation

"My advice to every restoration professional out there? Don't just read this. Follow it. Take his Restoration Millionaire Method™, implement it wherever you are in your business. Then, grow like crazy, enjoying all the extra time you don't have to spend figuring it all out the old-fashioned way. Be what Maxwell said: the wisest person, the one who learns from others' successes."

—Dan Martell, author of Wall Street Journal-bestseller *Buy Back Your Time*

"Restoration Millionaire is a crucial read for anyone in the restoration industry. Whether you're at the start of your journey or looking to expand, this book serves as a detailed guide to success. Alex's ability to simplify intricate concepts into practical steps is outstanding. Highly recommended!"

— Rico Garcia, host of Restoration Domination and Founder of EcoTek Pro Restoration

FOREWORD

Dan Martell is the author of the Wall Street Journal*-bestseller,* Buy Back Your Time. *After founding, scaling, and successfully exiting 3 technology companies, he was named Canada's top angel investor in 2012. A few years later, Dan founded SaaS Academy, now one of the world's largest coaching companies. He's also an Ironman athlete, philanthropist, husband, and father of 2 incredible boys.*

Legendary author and leader John C. Maxwell wrote this:

"A wise person learns from his mistakes. A wiser one learns from others' mistakes. But the wisest person of all learns from *others' successes.*"[1]

That's what you're holding in your hands (or listening to on your run): A collection of restoration successes, not only from my friend Alex Duta, but from other powerhouses in the industry. What's more? This book puts their stories together, to give you concrete strategies and tactics so you can learn from their successes to build your own amazing restoration company.

This industry, and others like it, are near and dear to my heart—several of my childhood friends now run local services companies, in emergency services, plumbing, electrical, carpentry, and other fields. I've seen firsthand the challenges they face finding resources on how to create better cashflow, how to implement a world-class referral program, or how to build standardized procedures. Few books, technologies, or podcasts solve these problems for restoration owners. Until now.

Having a problem with cashflow? Implement Alex's 48-Hour Rule™ for invoicing. Not sure how to create a world-class referral

---

[1] John C. Maxwell, *Leadership Gold: Lessons I've Learned from a Lifetime of Leading,* emphasis mine.

program? Use CIRCLS. Missing the systems, procedures, or checklists to execute consistently? Check out chapter eight.

This book is full of models and systems you can use right now—from the overall Restoration Millionaire Method™ Alex offers, to his CREDIT system for building a cash cushion, this book has the step-by-step answers I wish my childhood friends could have copied far earlier in their careers.

All of his advice, will save you time:

What if I told you that for a couple hours today, you could save yourself years of mistakes in this industry? What if I offered you the chance to copy, step-by-step, one of restoration's most innovative, hard-working, family-oriented leaders? What if I handed you the playbook to grow your business into the profitable millions, all while skipping costly errors?

That's what Alex is offering.

Whether you're at $50 million, or just starting out, Alex is offering you a method. A system. A plan to follow to solve problems, scale faster, and enjoy life more.

You can spend frustrating years cracking the codes of this industry, or you can invest a couple hours *now,* buy your future, and fast-forward to higher profits, more time with your family, and greater joy.

Alex and I have the same heartbeat for all entrepreneurs: We know they're the job-creators, the problem-solvers, the business-builders that the world depends on. We've both dedicated much of our lives to providing the missing support founders and business leaders need to lead successful lives *without* becoming overworked, stressed-out, and burnt out. Alex and I share a core philosophy:

Entrepreneurs *can* build successful businesses while being present with their families and enjoying the climb up the mountain, *if* they can find the right tactics, strategies, and playbooks.

This is one such playbook.

My advice to every restoration professional out there? Don't just read this. Follow it. Take his Restoration Millionaire Method™, implement it wherever you are in your business. Then, grow like crazy, enjoying all the extra time you *don't* have to spend figuring it all out the old-fashioned way. Be what Maxwell said: the wisest person, the one who learns from others' successes.

—Dan Martell, author of *Wall Street Journal*-bestseller *Buy Back Your Time*

To Laura & Sofia. You're my everything.

TABLE OF CONTENTS

$0-1 MILLION: (RE)SET THE FOUNDATION

CHAPTER 1:
The Reactive Rollercoaster™

New Tool

In this chapter, we're going to discuss the Reactive Rollercoaster™ that many restoration business owners find themselves riding. It's an ever-reactive wave of ups and downs. We're also going to discuss how to get off this rollercoaster with a basic business model: Set, Prove, Replicate

What you don't want:

What you do want:

- *<u>Set</u> (or reset) the foundation:* Whether you're just starting out in restoration, or you're an industry pro who has eight or more figures in revenue, you must learn how to set a foundation in your day-to-day operations so that your whole company can improve upon it.

- *Prove the model:* Once the foundation's set, it's time to prove (and improve) the business model with metrics, standard operating procedures, and other elements that can be duplicated.
- *Replicate & scale:* Once you've refined your business processes, you simply need to do it multiple times, over and over!

Can I ask you an honest question?

Does it ever feel like you're on a rollercoaster in your business, or even just in your life? As if you're not the one who's operating the controls, but you're just along for the ride? Sometimes it's scary, sometimes you're having a blast, waving your hands up in the air, and sometimes you find yourself just hanging on for dear life, but in the end, the whole ride is outside your control—do you feel that way?

Everyone feels this way from time to time, but if you own your own business (or you're considering starting one), you may feel this way *most* of the time: One day, the bank account's full, you're signing jobs, and all is well. Twenty-four hours later, a key employee quits, an insurance check goes sideways, a vendor fails to deliver, and all that good work that you just signed yesterday needs to get done *now.*

I'm from the restoration industry—where we're cleaning carpets, mitigating floods and fires, and helping build and rebuild homes—and here, for a long time, nearly every day felt like a rollercoaster to me. One day, I was working on a flooded basement, and the next, I was haggling with an insurance company; the next day, I was speaking with a nice, senior lady about why her cat peeing on her carpet isn't exactly covered by her homeowner's insurance.

Being on a rollercoaster is an odd feeling. It's exciting at times, but it's completely outside your control: someone else built the tracks, someone else buckles you in, and another person is operating the control panel. *You* have no control.

I have good news: Owning a business, or at least a restoration business, doesn't have to be that way. I want to help you get off the rollercoaster ride, and I want to help you get *into* the pilot's seat of your own life.

Simply put, there's a better way to run a restoration company, one that gives you the control of your business. I've been really lucky, in that I've had the opportunity to befriend, coach, and advise over a hundred different restoration-company owners in the United States and Canada. I've gotten to know the ins-and-outs of some of the biggest players in the market, like ATI Restoration, ServPRO, and others. I've also been on the ground-level with owners from smaller outfits doing anything from their first job, to $20 million a year in restoration work. And of course, I've owned my own restoration company, which I like to think is one of Chicagoland's best companies—Romexterra.

That's how I know exactly what being on the Reactive Rollercoaster™ feels like. It can feel like you're stuck because that's exactly how I felt a few years ago.

A Little of My Story

I started out in restoration for the same reasons most of us do—it was an easy industry to break into and make good money in, even for an immigrant like me. I'd come from Romania with my parents in 1998. When we left, my mom and dad were doing well there. After the fall of Communism, the country had a quick infusion of free-market idealism, and trade opened up. My parents may not have had a ton of money, but they were pretty quick on their toes—they started scooping up discarded pens, T-shirts, hats... anything that manufacturers who were working for Western companies were throwing away because of small defects. They would then resell these items in Romania for a small profit. (You'd be surprised how much a T-shirt that says "United American *Status*" can sell for in Romania!)

Later, my family ended up, quite literally, winning the immigration lottery. My parents packed up and moved the family away from their upper-middle-class life in Romania and started "at the bottom" in

America. By the time I was eighteen, my family had experienced a ton of financial ups and downs (kind of like a rollercoaster). So, experiencing those financial highs and lows, I grew up as a teenager promising myself repeatedly, *I'm going to be rich no matter what.*

When the opportunity came for me to go into business with my father at eighteen in a new restoration company, I dove in head-first.

Like many other restorers, builders, and contractors, I'd found that the restoration industry provides a rewarding environment—a business I could own, one that was relatively easy and inexpensive to start, and one that also had a quick return. In restoration, you can sign up for a huge, big-ticket job on Monday, then find the subcontractors to do the job (or even do all the work yourself!) that same day, then finish the work and be billing the insurance company by Friday!

Like many restorers, this is how I lived, and thought: sell a job, do a job, bill a job, collect on a job—it was a bit of a rollercoaster ride.

By the time I was twenty-one, I'd kept my promise to myself, and I had a couple commas in the bank. But, I'd kept my promise *too* well. I had done whatever it took to get rich. I had no real friends and no girlfriend, and I barely even spoke with my family outside of work. Without any real relationships, my mental health eventually took a plunge, and one day I landed in a hospital on suicide watch.

I know that's a bit dramatic, but don't worry—my family not only stepped in, but they stepped up to regain their important roles in my life. That was almost a decade ago. Today, I've ensured that relationships are one of the central ingredients in my life. I'm married to an amazing woman, and we have a beautiful daughter. But, that doesn't take away from the seriousness of that episode.

You see, even though I'd started a great, award-winning restoration company that had scaled into the seven figures by the time I was twenty-one, I'd never learned how to truly juggle everything. I didn't understand how to create a business that I loved, one that provided a stable income while allowing me freedom and control over my life and time.

There's a lot of reasons why I hadn't learned those lessons, but one of them is this: There aren't a ton of conferences, podcasts, books, or heck, even *blogs* for restorers on how to run their companies. You can go to school to be a doctor, a lawyer, or even a mechanical engineer. You can easily find a dozen or more *New York Times*-bestselling books by top authors on how to invest, how to make money in real estate, or how to be a corporate CEO. But where do you go to learn about emergency services, mitigation, or construction rebuilds? Us restorers are sort of left completely to fend for ourselves.

Don't worry, I'm on a mission to change that, not only at my current venture-backed company, Albi, but also, with this book.

That's right: you're holding one of the few resources in the world designed with *you* in mind.

The Reactive Rollercoaster™

For me, my Reactive Rollercoaster™ was mostly mental, physical, and relational. I'd pay attention to one thing, at the expense of another. Sometimes, I'd sacrifice my mental health for my finances. Other times, I'd focus on my finances, while my relationships took a toll. Eventually, I'd do better in my personal relationships, but I'd forget all about my physical health. In fact, I allowed my weight to skyrocket to over 220 pounds at one point—*way* too much for a guy of my height. (I won't tell you exactly how tall I am, but I will remind you that Tom Cruise is one of the most handsome guys on the planet, and he's only 5' 7"!)

Up and down, up and down, like a yo-yo.

And it wasn't just *outside* my business that felt like a rollercoaster, but it was inside my own mind: It felt as if I was constantly juggling too many balls, and I always had to decide which one I was going to catch. For instance, in the early stages of Romexterra, I was at the center of the entire business, and every problem and issue passed through me. Not only was I selling, but I was managing projects on the ground, plus, I was recruiting, hiring, firing, and collecting. I was on a rollercoaster—one problem solved, another ball dropped.

I've seen the same thing, time and time again with other restorers. I can tell you stories about Jack, who was doing quite well in the industry (he was making millions!), but he felt burned out. I could tell you about Steven, who had addiction problems, and went from millions in revenue, to asking me for a salaried job as a manager. I could tell you about George, who never really got his business off the ground, even after years of struggling.

Some restorers have no money; others have plenty. But in almost every case, I can spot a trend in their company, and it looks like this: One month, they're focusing on sales but dropping the ball on hiring. So, the next, they react to that and focus on hiring better staff. Of course, while they're focusing on hiring, they forget about all the work they just signed that should be getting done, so projects start slipping. In reaction to that, they start managing all the work, but now, the new employees aren't getting trained properly, so they start focusing on training them. Meanwhile, they're failing to collect on all the jobs they just completed. So, they then rush to collect checks, but then, since no one's doing sales, they start selling again, and thus, the cycle begins again:

The Reactive Rollercoaster

Reactivity Vs. Proactivity

Does that rollercoaster resemble your business? Maybe you need to delete the words on the image, and just think about how you *feel:* Does it feel like you have a lot of emotional highs, followed by dark lows? Does it feel like you're just along for the ride, hoping that the next big drop doesn't throw you out of the cart?

Restorers aren't alone in this feeling. It's actually pretty common for *all* entrepreneurs, at some level. Manfred F.R. Kets de Vries, a Dutch business management scholar and consultant, has been studying businesses for decades. In 1985, he wrote this in a *Harvard Business Review* article:[2]

> *Entrepreneurs somehow know how to lead an organization and give it momentum. Along with their mystique, however, entrepreneurs can have personality quirks that make them hard people to work with. For example,* ***their bias toward action,*** *which* ***makes them act rather thoughtlessly,*** *sometimes can have dire consequences for the organization.*[2]

In his *Wall Street Journal* bestseller *Buy Back Your Time,* serial entrepreneur (and my mentor!) Dan Martell talks about the "addiction to chaos" that many entrepreneurs experience.

So, on one hand, us restorers are pretty normal for the business world. But on the other hand, I actually think we have it worse. I mean, think about it: We're reactive, by nature, because we are in a very, very reactive industry. We're constantly responding to emergencies, like floods or fires, and oftentimes, we're taking a customer's call at 2 a.m., just after a tragedy has struck. In fact, many of us get into the restoration industry, because we're just the sorts of people who are quick-thinkers who can respond to stressful situations with some creativity.

Plus, many of us are attracted to the other aspects of the industry:

1) There's a quick return on money. You can get in, start a business, find the subcontractors, sign a job, all in a day or two without any capital investment.

2) You get to be the hero. By helping customers in their biggest time of need with one of their most precious physical assets (their homes), you can make positive changes in countless people's lives. You can save the cat from a flooded basement, replace old

---

[2] Bolding mine.

water-damaged countertops with gorgeous granite ones, or clean a woman's carpets the day before Christmas.

3) This industry is recession-proof. There will always be emergencies, most of which are covered by insurance companies.

4) Not much competition. Very few kids are going around saying, "I want to be in restoration when I grow up!"

So, yes—restoration is a great industry, with high profit margins, low barriers to entry, with very little red tape. But the bad news is... we can all end up stressed, overworked, and on a rollercoaster someone else designed, where we end up simply reacting to the world around us.

Reactivity is one way of running your company. But, there's another way, one that allows you to be proactive, to make decisions on your own, take control of your life and execute what *you* think is important.

Don't take it from me, take it from one of my competitors:

When my father and I started Romexterra in Chicagoland in 2014, another company, a competitor, started about the same. We were able to grow ours to over eight figures in about six years. Meanwhile, that competitor? They had almost *five times the growth rate we had.* And they did it with a proactive plan.

Our competitor started out with a fantastic business model that allowed them to grow rapidly—they paid almost every person in their restoration company a percentage. A salesperson would make about 10 percent, a project manager would make around 6, and a crew chief also made around 10 percent. This allowed our competitor to proactively manage cashflow—one of the biggest problems in the industry.

They also ensured that they tied the important metrics of their operation to those paychecks and percentages. For instance, let's say that a crew chief finished a job for $20,000, and they made 10 percent of that. Well, later, if an insurance company only paid out $19,000 on the job, the crew chief would have a future paycheck adjusted for $100 less, accounting for the difference. [3] Pretty soon, every crew chief and project manager was very, very good at documentation, estimating, and collecting payments. Again, our competitor proactively handled two of the biggest pain points in the industry—ensuring that all employees bill correctly, and that they send invoices on time.

This company started the same time as my father and I did, and by the time I exited Romexterra, our competitor was operating somewhere around nine figures.

We'll talk about the specifics in the rest of the book, but the point I'm trying to make is *not* about paying percentage or documentation. Rather, I'm trying to point out that our competitor had the foresight to proactively handle almost all of the industry's biggest problems.

And do you know what? They were right: Proactivity isn't just an option. It's a necessity for fields that exist within high-stakes environments.

Think about it: There are *lots* of industries that are, by nature, reactive like restoration and emergency services. Consider an actual emergency room, with doctors, nurses, surgeons, and other medical staff. Imagine if they all reacted to every situation with no plan in mind, as if every time someone walked in with a heart attack, gunshot wound, or broken arm, the medical staff responded with, *Let's figure this out on the fly!* Would *you* want to visit such a hospital? No way. A hospital that was dealing with everything as if it were an improv class would be in utter chaos.

Instead, while they work very hard and very quickly, medical personnel inside of hospitals typically have plans for every situation. They know how to prioritize what injuries and illnesses, who to call, and what to do. They're proactive.

The same thing is true in another high-stakes industry, aviation. The aviation industry has more at stake than even restoration, and there are just as many (if not more!) elements outside the control of the pilot—

---

[3] 10 percent of $1,000 = $100

bad weather, erratic passengers, mechanical failures, and a long, long list of other complications that make flying a very dangerous game. But pilots aren't reactive. Instead, they're *proactive:* Pilots submit flight plans before they fly. They go over pre-flight checklists when they step into the cockpit. When they're in the air, pilots have very, very specific procedures for each and every scenario— "If I stall out, do x, y, and z." "If there's bad weather, do a, b, and c." Checklists, playbooks, procedures, all for very volatile, highly unpredictable scenarios.

Wouldn't it be amazing if your restoration business had similar game plans? If you knew exactly what to do, when? If there was an actual, tested plan you could follow to make *predictable* cashflow in your restoration company?

Well, what if I told you that you can have similar peace-of-mind? What if I told you there is a plan you can follow to build a kick-ass referral program that constantly brings in new business? What if I showed you how to hire the right people, and then put them in the right positions to handle problems without your involvement?

Well, guess what? You're holding the book with *all* of that information. From marketing to cashflow, from referral programs to making your first million, from how to set up your shop, to how to organize your company—you're holding *the* resource with tested checklists, playbooks, and procedures. This book can help you land your first restoration job, and the information here will help you keep growing, even after you've hit seven figures, or eight in your restoration company.

I know that's true because I'm not on a rollercoaster anymore. I learned how to become what I call "a proactive pilot," one that flies according to their own, predetermined flight plan. One who picks their own travel destination. Today, I use procedures, planning, and even the experiences of others to navigate business and life.

The Rest of My Story

After my health scare in the hospital, and after I reconnected with my family, I started reading, learning, and understanding how to run a business. Sure, I already knew how to make sales and increase revenue, but I wanted to be a leader with a plan—a proactive pilot instead of a Reactive Rollercoaster™-rider. I read hundreds of books on business (and I couldn't even find *one* specifically written for restoration, by the way!). I consumed hundreds of hours of podcasts, audio books, and YouTube videos. I spent $100,000 a year on the best business coaches. I borrowed the best plans from others. I doubled- and tripled-down on what was already working at my fast-growing company. I looked anywhere I could to find out how to grow faster, be smarter, and find more balance.

What I learned ultimately enabled me to empower my employees. I started adding metrics that created incentives, so others performed their work accurately. I put up boundaries, even for our emergency services team, so that we weren't all on our toes every evening hoping for a late-night call that would land us that next big job. I can honestly say, I found the answers I was looking for to become a proactive leader, not a reactive, "hold on tight and hope for the best" type of person.

You can do the same—you can find your answers. One option is to read dozens of books, watch and listen to hours and hours of content, make plenty of mistakes, and hire all the best coaches. That's what I did. You could do all that, *or*, instead, you could read this book: I've taken all that I've learned, and more, and put it into this one special resource. Importantly, I've written this asset for us, for the *restorers.* While I had to wade through books on real estate, investing, and marketing to glean the best tips, tricks, and plans to fuel my own company's growth, then implement them, and iterate on them, *you* can find what I think is the best information, right here, in one place. Tested, and verified, just for restorers.

As I learned how to become the pilot of my own restoration company, others in the industry started noticing. While I'd always made money, I also started becoming happy, and a great family man. (Well, I don't know about "great," but my wife says I do alright!). My good friends in the restoration industry started coming to me for advice—some were just starting out, others had eight-figure companies.

You'll learn about some of their stories as we go along (but I'll probably change their names, you know, to protect the innocent!), but first, I'm an action guy. While I like stories, I like to learn something. So, let's talk about the first, most important lesson. It's one we're going to come back to a lot in this book, because it needs lots of repetition for something to sink in. It's called Set, Prove, Rep.

Set, Prove, Rep

Let's go back to that story about our competitor—the one that started out their company with the percentage-based structure, then scaled up and absolutely killed it. Our competitor had a flight plan, a path to follow from the beginning, one that allowed them to scale. Again, I call this Set, Prove, Rep:

First, our competitor developed a foundational model with a great plan that would allow them to grow into the future. That model was their percentage-based pay-structure. That model ensured they would never be upside-down with their cashflow.

Next, as our competitor grew, they had to make adjustments where necessary, and even add in metrics and documentation that ensured alignment (like the paycheck adjustments).

Finally, our competitor continued to replicate and scale that same model across the company.

That's the three-step, Set, Prove, Rep plan of action we can all take, now. And it's not unique to restoration—it's a plan of action every business can utilize.

In software, for instance, we do something similar: First, we build out a software (set), then, we make sure it actually works, by fixing all the bugs and asking our customers if the tool we've built is usable (prove). Then, once everything looks great, we expand the company to as many people as we can (replicate).

You'll find this same three-step plan *almost everywhere* that experiences growth, even in nature: An acorn tree lays its roots then attempts to sprout high. Along the way, it withstands storms, bugs, and pests. Once it's matured, it drops more acorns, and the process begins again. Bacteria, animals, and even the way galaxies come together follows the same path—Set, Prove, Rep.

You could use this simple three-step philosophy to solve a problem *right now* in your restoration company. Let's say you're making $10 million a year, and your biggest problem is documentation—every project manager is handling their end-of-job documentation entirely differently (or maybe, they're not handling it at all!). Using Set, Prove, Rep, you could solve this problem:

One way would be to write down a simple checklist that you want every project manager to follow for every project (set).

Then, you could give that checklist to your top project managers, asking them to fill it out for a month and give you feedback in the process to make sure you didn't miss anything (prove).

Once that checklist is nearly perfect, you could implement that template across the company for every project, every time (replicate).

Boom—using Set, Prove, Rep, your documentation problem would be solved in thirty days or less.

How This Book Is Laid Out

In the rest of this book, we're going to go over every area of your restoration business—from cashflow management, to marketing, to gaining new customers, to referrals. I'll give you playbooks, checklists, and procedures on how to handle *every* problem, with plenty of detail. We'll talk about the 48-Hour Rule™, a plan that helps you solve one of the biggest problems in the industry—getting paid on time. I'll tell you about the Jack & George brains, the two key ways of thinking, both of which you must have available within your company. I'll explain "Fishing Holes" and how to make your first million, or your next $10 million.

But if you want to get started right now, you just need to know one key thing: Set, Prove, Rep. That simple concept is the powerful, 1-2-3 punch you need to change the game in your business, to go from being a Reactive Rollercoaster™-rider, to a proactive pilot. And speaking of the rest of the book, I've actually laid it out that way, following the Set, Prove, Rep model:

I. **$0-1 MILLION: (RE)SET THE FOUNDATION:** In the first part of the book, we'll talk about how to make money, and how to collect cash, fast. In this part, we'll also solve several of your ongoing business problems—likely problems you've faced time and time again, but no one bothered to give you the easy tools to solve them. I've labeled this section "$0-1 MILLION," but even if your restoration company is already making $50 million, I've found that most restoration owners who are struggling in their company, may need to "reset" small pieces of their foundation.

II. **$1-5 MILLION: PROVE THE MODEL:** Next, in the second part of this book, we'll talk about fine-tuning your business processes and figuring out how to implement operating procedures and company-wide metrics that allow *others,* besides *you,* the owner, to take responsibility. Here, you'll also find out how to use simple organizational charts (ones that are actually helpful), and we'll discuss my Ten Commandments of Hiring, Firing, and Inspiring.

III. **$5 MILLION+: REPLICATE & SCALE:** The last part of this book will go over how to build a cash cushion, so that you can take on huge jobs, even if you don't have the trucks, equipment, or manpower immediately available. You'll also find out where to spend your time, strategically, so you can make more and more money as your company continues to scale.

The money I attached to these phases are very general; I spoke with several industry experts, and many of them put the numbers at different levels. In other words, while mine are a bit of an average, some people have foundational issues at $10 million; others seem to have a "scaling" problem at a lower level. So, keep these numbers very loose in your head, and recognize feelings and problems more than just the numbers.

No Man's Land

In between each phase, there's a bit of a "no man's land," where you're too big to be at one level, but too small to be in the next. Often, what happens at these junctures is you have to lean into pain and take risks to move forward. For instance, you may not have quite enough money to buy a new truck or hire a key leader, but without doing so, you won't be able to grow. Or perhaps you won't quite have all your processes down pat, but you know you need to grow a little more and move into a new location, even though you're still proving your model. When you hit these junctures, it's important to lean *forward* not backward, because whatever isn't growing, is dying.

The Proactive Pilot

Today, I'm not on a rollercoaster, with my health, my wealth, my spirituality, or my business. I'm a pilot now. As in, a real *pilot,..* like, I've learned how to fly a plane. This has helped me understand that there really are playbooks and procedures for *everything.* In aviation, those procedures, checklists, and playbooks help me predict outcomes—I know how to fly from one town to another, how to land an aircraft in darkness, when and where to refuel, and a whole list of other flying practices.

In restoration, we have the same opportunities. There are playbooks for everything—how to do better marketing, how to pull cash forward, how to make your customers happy, how to start a kick-ass referral program, along with a bunch of tips, tricks, and tactics that work without fail. The difference between aviation and restoration is that there isn't a governing body with a bunch of big words that gives you a license to become a restorer. So, if it's helpful, consider this book the "FAA" of restoration. And, in each chapter, we'll discuss specific problem areas, then lay out a specific tool you can use to solve it.

My guess is, you became a restorer the same way most of us did—you had a family to feed, and you went out and made it happen. Now, there are many problems no one told you about, and it feels like you're on the Reactive Rollercoaster™—money in, money out, problem today, fire tomorrow.

No more Reactive Rollercoaster™ rides for you; I want you to be a proactive pilot.

Here's to flying.

Momentum Trigger

In this book, we're going to talk a ton about momentum. Every chapter will end with a tactical action plan that you can implement ***right now.***

For this first chapter, we're going to make the Momentum Trigger simple. I want you to write down the problems you're facing right now—the ones that make you feel like you're on the Reactive Rollercoaster™, and I want you to make a promise to yourself that you're going to read and implement what you learn so you can solve these problems. Plenty of studies show that when write down goals, we're more likely to accomplish them.[4] So even if it feels awkward, let's just go for it.

[4] Murphy, Mark. "Neuroscience Explains Why You Need to Write down Your Goals If You Actually Want to Achieve Them." Forbes, September 12, 2023

First, write down your one to three biggest problems you're facing:

1: ____

2: ____

3: ____

Then, make a promise to yourself that you will *implement* what you learn to attack those problems. Put it in your own words (it's your book; go ahead and write in it!).

____

____

*Note: If you want a clean sheet, an electronic version of this tactic, or any other homework throughout the book, you can head to RestorationMillionaire.com/Resources and find all the tools we discuss in this book, and more. We're here for you!

Restorer's Recap

We'll end each chapter discussion with a recap, just for us restorers (sort of like how we end each job by getting a certificate of completion from our clients, detailing the work performed).

Here's what we talked about in this chapter:

- Restoration is an easy industry to break into. That's why it's so attractive to hustlers, hard-working immigrants, and those who don't want to work a traditional job.
- Many people in restoration end up on the Reactive Rollercoaster™, whether in their business, or their personal life. They learn to constantly solve one problem—like hiring more people, better project management, or cashflow issues—only to end up in another problem. However, there's a better way; it's called *proactivity.*
- The proactive pilot: it's possible to seize control and have predictable outcomes, even in the restoration industry. Other fields, like aviation or emergency healthcare, have highly specific guidebooks that help individuals execute predictable outcomes. In this book, we're going to learn tested playbooks, procedures, and checklists that have worked for hundreds and thousands of other restorers.

- The first tool you have to solve any business problem is Set, Prove, Rep:
    - Set: First, set up a possible solution that will lead to the outcome you want.
    - Prove: Next, iterate on the solution you've created.
    - Rep: Once you've determined that your solution works, replicate your plan.

CHAPTER 2:
Jack & George

"If it hadn't been for my big brother, I swear I'd have been in jail several times for check-bouncing."
—Walt Disney

New Tool

In this chapter, we're going to learn about the two personas in business, the two types of people that I call "Jacks" and "Georges."[5] I'll refer to them throughout the book, with the following icons:

Jacks are fast-moving, smooth-talking salespeople who know how to get sh*t done! If you're a Jack, you hustle and grow your business fast, but you often ignore the importance of operational procedures. Jacks typically scale their businesses quickly, but they often stall at a certain point because there are no procedures in place.

[5] I didn't want anyone thinking that women or men were more likely to be a Jack or George, so I made them both male. But, if you're a lady reading this, you could change both to "Jackie" and "Georgina" if you'd prefer!

Georges are the opposite—they're often operationally and procedurally flawless but not the best with sales. A Georges' company could scale infinitely, because they have all because they have all the right procedures in place, they make great decisions, hire the right people,.. the only problem is, they don't have many sales coming in.

You need both brains in your business to scale successfully. You should be authentic, meaning you should embrace whether you're a Jack or a George, but at the same time, you must develop the "other side" of your brain in your company, through training, hires, etc.

"Absolutely not. Our restoration company's not going to spend $500 on a lead. That's a scam," said my father, in a way only a Romanian immigrant born under Communist rule could.

I nodded, agreeing not to work with the lead-generating company that charged $500 for every estimate our company landed from them. At least that's what my father thought my nodding meant (and what I wanted him to think).

But then, I secretly called them back and threw down my own credit card. I know; it was a bit of a bold move, but I was only nineteen, and our new company, Romexterra, hadn't sold a single restoration job yet. *What was the worst that could happen?* I thought.

I hung up the phone, then sat up all night pacing and staring at my phone, waiting for that one lead to come in that would change our company's destiny forever.

I know... it sounds a little absurd. And you're probably thinking, *Alex is crazy.* Well, you're probably right. I am a little crazy. But I think to be an entrepreneur, you have to be, right?

You see, from day one, I had that entrepreneurial "stuff." Maybe you do, too. Maybe you're a tough and hungry go-getter who's action-oriented. Or maybe, necessity simply forced you into starting your own small business. For me, it was a little bit of both...

When I was a teenager, I was throwing up websites for customers around town who owned small businesses. One of my website clients, a snow-removal company, kept tossing all his residential leads because he only did commercial snow-removal jobs, so I offered to take on the smaller gigs. He agreed, even throwing in his own truck to get my new "business" off the ground. (So thankful that you believed in me, Matt Bando!)

Before I knew it, I was leading a team of half a dozen other high schoolers, pulling all-nighters to shovel snow, then bee-lining it to school by morning to try and not fall asleep in my biology class. By the time I was a senior in high school, my little business had multiple routes, half a dozen trucks, and was servicing upwards of 150 homes.[6]

I didn't know it then, but the restoration bug was about to bite me, hard!

Before graduation, I took a vacation with my parents. As we walked along the beach, I got a glimpse into my dad's personality. By then, he was a construction employee, but he was looking to jump back into the entrepreneurial game.

Risen from a small house with no water or electricity in Communist Romania, he married my middle-class mom, then started selling B-class pens, T-shirts, etc., after the fall of Communism. When we moved to America, my dad worked whatever job was necessary to make money for us, and eventually took a job in construction. But he honestly wanted to get back into his own company.

On the beach, he was telling me his plan of opening a restaurant. Seemingly, he had it all figured out—he had all the numbers, the ideas, and the plans. I listened with intensity to my dad's plan. I started

---

[6] Sidenote: if you're reading this and haven't started your restoration company yet, snow plowing is one of those oft-overlooked cashflow-heavy enterprises that's perfect for a first-time entrepreneur (particularly if you're young and hungry!).

understanding something about him and me: While he wanted to own his own company again, he was getting older, and less OK with taking risks. He was never really a salesperson, but he *was* fantastic at making sure everything operated well. I mean, look how much time he'd spent putting together the restaurant plan? I would *never* have thought to "plan" much of anything!

I started thinking, *you know, my snow-removal "company" isn't really going anywhere big. Maybe I could link up with my dad...*

So, being the young guy I was, I just threw it out there:

"Dad, isn't *all* of your experience in restorative construction? Why not start a business like that?"

"There's a list of reasons, son. Besides all the regulations and insurance requirements, I'm not a salesman, and landing jobs in this industry is very, very difficult."

And that's when I went in for the big question:

"But dad, do you know what? *I'm* a salesperson! I've sold over a hundred homes in my snow-removal service! You know what I'm *not* good at? All this operational stuff that you know how to do well!"

I paused.

"Dad, why don't we join forces? Selling a restoration job is far more lucrative than selling a snow-shoveling gig. Plus, you know about all this restoration construction stuff. I'll handle the front-end sales; you handle the back-end logistics. What do you say?"

So, right there on the beach, Alex and Alex's dad shook on it. We were officially in business as "Romexterra."

We started our little company with a few basic goals: Sell two fires a year, do most of the work ourselves, then each walk away with $100,000 in our pockets. That sounded great to me, but four months in, I—the teenage sales prodigy—had sold exactly zero fires. I'd chased ambulances, eavesdropped on fire scanners, shown up to homes minutes after first responders... over 100 times, and still? Not a single fire.

Every time I showed up at a house after a fire, five or six other salespeople did the same thing, and they were all from bigger companies. The firefighters pretty much hated us—they saw us as the cockroaches of the industry, worthless ambulance-chasers taking advantage of distraught homeowners, moments after a tragedy.

While I didn't sell anything, I did notice something. I observed that all the companies who *did* win jobs were branded a little bit differently. They didn't bill themselves as "rebuilders," but rather, they showed up in vans that said, "emergency services," in big, bright letters on the sides of their vehicles. Instead of trying to sell rebuilds, they offered to help board up homes, clean homeowners' clothes, and remove any salvageable furniture. Amazingly, those emergency restoration companies didn't just win the immediate, emergency work, they'd *also* win the fire rebuild, what most of us were really after.

So, I decided to rebrand our company to provide emergency services, which brings us right back to me pacing in my bedroom all night, waiting for the phone to ring...

The lead-generation company I'd signed up with was called Spark87[7], and they were a marketing company that worked specifically by connecting homeowners with restoration companies on a commission-only basis. If a homeowner wanted an estimate, the restoration company would pay Spark $500. Otherwise, Spark got nothing. I loved that idea (even though my dad had called them a "scam." So, that night, right after I'd signed up, I stayed up all night pacing the floor, staring at my phone, half-awake, until about 5 am. I was just waiting and hoping for that phone call with a hot lead that would change my destiny.

Now, you're probably thinking, *Of course this story ends without Alex getting a single lead the **first night**.*

But you know what? It went better than that—I got *five* leads! A single flood had knocked out eight homes, and I ended up on the phone with five of those homeowners, *all* of whom wanted estimates. I immediately drove out to each house. Lo and behold, I walked away with five signatures!

---

[7] Not their real name.

Now, that was the easy part. Then, I had a lot of explaining to do with my dad. If I was going to wake up a grumpy Romanian dad, I was going to lead with the good parts of the story.

"Hey dad! Sorry to call you so early... I just signed *$60,000* worth of work for us!"

My dad was excited. He woke up in his whitey-tighties, and then woke up *his* dad, who happened to be visiting from Romania. Then, I called my buddy, who was doing yard cleanup. I offered to triple his hourly pay if he'd drop everything and come help me. He showed up with *his* dad. After a few more calls, I'd wrangled together a seven-man team before most people were out of bed, and we all worked for nineteen hours straight that first day.

After a couple days, we'd finished all five of the homes. A few days later, I collected the checks, and paid out our "employees." My dad and I walked out with about $10,000 *each!*

*This is **way** better than snow removal!* I thought. But, my dad had a question:

"How in the world did you get those leads?!" he asked.

"Oh, you know that lead-gen company you said not to use? I used them."

OK, I just have to tell you the rest of the story, because it gets better.

Not only did we win the $60,000 in mitigation work, but because we had our foot in the door with the homeowners, we ended up with a majority of the reconstruction, too. That one decision to work with Spark87 led to a month's worth of work for Romexterra!

Salespeople vs. Operational Gurus

Over the next few years, my dad and I would work together in a bit of a similar fashion—I would come up with a crazy idea, and he would try to reign me in. A lot of the time, I was right, and the same goes for him.

I learned something through my working relationship with my father—that we needed each other, or, more accurately, our business needed the personality of the person. My sales-brain needed someone who understood logistics and operations, and my dad's brain needed someone with a little fire in the belly who could take risks and land work, even without everything totally figured out. My partnership with my father at Romexterra was only successful because we had both types of thinking present, and because we listened to each other. Now, of course, we often frustrated each other, too. But in the end, the magic was found somewhere in the middle of our two ways of thinking—he needed me to push the company forward, to take risks, to hustle new sales, ideas, and partnerships. I needed him to ensure there were actually dollars in the bank!

You know what's wild? Is that it's just not me and my dad. Lots of companies have this same sort of partnership, with someone who's the hungry go-getter, and someone who's the down-to-Earth realist, who actually makes sure the company doesn't go off the rails. Sometimes, it happens like it did with my dad and me—where one person is the "salesperson," and the other is the "operational" person. At Apple, Steve Jobs was the visionary go-getter, and Steve "The Woz" Wozniak actually put together a lot of the computers and did the engineering.

In some companies, it takes more than two people to put these components together. For instance, At Rolls-Royce, there was the race-car-driving Charles Rolls, and the hard-working engineer Henry Royce, but there was *also* another guy named Claude "CJ" Johnson. Many people called CJ the "hyphen in Rolls-Royce." According to many, CJ was the real brains behind the company. Together, this trio had salesmanship, business acumen, and a stellar product that continues to wow audiences to this day.

One of the coolest stories about the need for both of these types of thinking is actually found in the Walt Disney Company, about the brothers, Walt Disney and Roy Disney. Walt was *all* vision. But, in his words, "If it hadn't been for my big brother, I swear I'd have been in jail several times for check-bouncing." While Walt was off dreaming up the next crazy idea, Roy was dotting the Is and crossing the Ts, ensuring the company had operational integrity.

Take a look at any of the greatest companies of our time, and you'll find vision and salesmanship coupled with operational excellency. On the other hand, when a company fails, it's often because one of these two types of personalities is missing.

Jack & George

I saw this dual-minded philosophy in real time when speaking with two of my real-life coaching clients. I don't want to use their real names, so we'll call them "Jack" and "George." First, there was Jack. He was a lot like me, and Walt, and Steve Jobs—he was a bit flashy, and he was *crushing* sales at his restoration company. But do you know what? He was *drowning* in problems, which is why he called me. His employees and subcontractors had little to no direction. All his accounting books were a total mess, meeting deadlines was a struggle, and collecting invoices on time was rare. Sales may have been really high, but so was his anxiety (and everyone else's on his team!). There were no standardized procedures, no handbooks, nothing was written down, and every job was completed as if it were the first time they'd ever done it. Honestly, Jack's company was in complete chaos.

The same week, I met with George. Much like my dad, this guy was an operational guru. He'd probably read all the good business books, from Gino Wickman's *What the Heck Is EOS?* to *The Checklist Manifesto* by Atul Gawande. He had reporting measures in place, great accounting, and a fantastic organizational chart so that all his employees knew exactly what to do and when to do it. Invoices were always collected on time, and every job was completed under-budget and within deadlines. All his employees really liked George, and their morale was high,.. but sales were not high. George was making very little money.

That week, meeting with both Jack and George, I had one of those "aha" moments that smack you right in the face. Once I saw their issues clearly, I could never *unsee* them. I'd heard of these problems for years, as I'd gotten to know hundreds of restoration owners and formally coached dozens of them. I'd usually helped them see each issue, and they would solve it. That was helpful, but something about Jack and George's issues made it so clear to me—every business needs some "Jack" and some "George" in them, if they want to succeed. If Jack could have borrowed some of George's business acumen, his employees would have been happy, processes would have become streamlined, and work would have been completed on time. On the other hand, if George could just steal some of Jack's stellar charisma, sales would go through the roof. Both were half an equation that was missing a critical component.

Few people (other than the real-life Jack and George!) represent one category or the other fully, at all times. What's more likely is that you *lean* more "Jack," or you *lean* more "George" at different times of your life, or in different situations. Do you like to move fast, sell jobs, and ignore details? You're probably more of a Jack. Do you love to think things through before making any rash moves, enjoy a plan really coming together, and often get bogged down in details? You're probably more of a George.

To be clear, I'm not telling you to go find your other half as a business partner. I don't think everyone needs to have a real, adult-sized Jack and George pair running around their offices. Rather, what I think we all need to do is recognize who we are, and what our strengths and weaknesses are, and then, find some way to borrow what we don't have.

Get a Little Jack & George Into Your Business

As I've aged (I mean, I'm not that old! As I write this, I'm only 27!), I've learned to take on more of my dad's George-like qualities. But still, even at my new venture, Albi, I went into it knowing I needed to solve the George-brain problem: I needed someone who would ensure my visionary craziness didn't ruin our company! I found my solution in Shamoil Soni, my cofounder. This guy has a top-notch IT degree and was a kick-ass software engineer... I can't say enough good things about him. He's a brutally hard worker, with absurd talents, *and* he's everything that I'm not. So, at Albi, I've added in the George-ness that I need by bringing on a cofounder, Shamoil, who's an absolute rockstar. Together, we're building what I think is the world's greatest software platform for restorers. We're ruthlessly dedicated to solving all the problems that restorers face, with a platform that helps track customer relationships, profitability, job-flow, and nearly everything else that a restorer could want to know, all in one, easy-to-use platform. OK, I'll stop now! I just love restorers and technology!

When I left my restoration company, Romexterra, to start Albi, my dad had a similar issue -- I was the Jack to his George. While I solved the two-brain-problem at my new company, Albi, by finding Shamoil, who's a George genius, my dad solved his lack-of-Jack problem by learning and developing his own sales acumen. The difference is important: you *don't* need both people in every partnership, by any means. What you need is both wings, both brains present, some way or the other.

You could add in both brains a lot of ways—hire more George geniuses or solve your lack-of-Jack with employees that *are* Jacks. Or, you could get a mentor who can point out your flaws. Or, you could read books, listen to podcasts, and work on your weaknesses while keeping your strengths.

There's a lot of ways to add both brains in your business. The method isn't important, but the outcome is. Simply put, you need to pepper your steak with the seasoning that's missing—what parts of the other brain do you need?

If you want to have a well-run business, you'll have to understand your own strengths and weaknesses, and fill in the missing pieces. And that's what I want you to have in this book—what you lack. The answer isn't "go partner up with your other half." Rather, it's to be honest about where you're at currently.

So, let's start, right now. (Like I said in the last chapter, I'm an action guy!) Take a look at the chart below, right now, and let's figure out whether you're more of a Jack or more of a George:

JACK *The Visionary*	GEORGE *The Operator*
Typically a great salesman	Often hates sales
Is usually charismatic, extroverted	Is typically more introverted
Usually thinks "big picture"	Often a product designer
Often skips details	Is detail-oriented
A hustler for new work	Is often called a "doer" or "executor"
Takes risk	Is often risk-averse
Rarely enjoys getting involved with the daily operations	Cares deeply about the daily operations of the business
Often thrives under pressure	Seeks ways to create a more peaceful, sound business
Often struggles keeping up with invoices, paperwork, employees, procedures, regulations, and administrative tasks	Excels with invoices, employees, procedures, regulations, and administrative paperwork
Steve Jobs	Steve Wozniak
Bill Gates	Paul Allen
Walt Disney	Roy Disney

So, which are you? Do you see yourself as having more Jack or more George in you? Remember, people often shift throughout their life, or morph in different scenarios.

I'm not Dr. Phil, and this isn't a true personality test. I'm telling you all this because it matters, and once you identify who and what you are, you can start to fill in your gaps with understanding. Typically, I've found, that a big reason restorers end up on the Reactive Rollercoaster™ I mentioned in chapter one, is because they're either all Jack or all George, and they don't realize it. So, they're missing out on the other half of what they need in every business to make it successful.

Throughout this book, every chapter should be helpful to both Jacks and Georges, but whenever there's something that a Jack or a George *really* needs to hear, just for them, you'll see a little callout with one of the following symbols:

That way, whether you're more of a Jack or a George, you can look at your icons and follow along. But, for now, I want to provide you a few practical things that both types can do:

1: Develop Yourself

Whether you're a Jack or George, here's something you can both do: start reading books, listening to podcasts, or watching helpful YouTube videos to cover any blind spots you may have.

While I've learned a ton from my own experiences, much of what I've learned throughout the years has been from other people who are great to follow. While other resources aren't going to say, "Hey Jack, listen up!" or "Hey George, this podcast is for you!" once you know who you are, you can go seek out resources that will help you smooth out your rough edges:

- For Jacks, you need to focus a *lot* on procedures, metrics, and operations. One great place to start for *you* would be by reading the book *Traction: Get a Grip on Your Business* by Gino Wickman.
- For Georges, focus on content that can help you bring in more sales. So, check out resources that focus on developing your sales pitch, your speaking skills, or overcoming your fear of talking about money. Dean Graziosi, a business partner of Tony Robbins, talks a lot about why selling your product is actually a loving act. Check out some of his YouTube videos for starters.

2: Hire More Jacks Or Georges

You don't need to give away half your company or bring on a business partner to get more of Jack's sales ability or more of George's operational mind. You can just hire more of what you need.

For instance, once you know that you're more of a George, you may want to ensure that your project managers have some amazing sales abilities. That way, as your revenue grows, you can step out of the sales roles and pass them off to your project managers. (A helpful clue for Georges: Jack-types are usually attracted to commission!)

Or, let's say you're more of a Jack. For you, make sure you have some very strong, operationally minded people on your team that you listen to, and you give a lot of power to. Once you're at a certain revenue level, you can actually "fire" yourself from certain jobs and hand those over to your office staff, your project managers, or others; that way, you can stay more focused on doing what you're good at—sales—without hurting the rest of your team with your disorganization.

Obviously, you'll only want to hire out sales or office management at the appropriate revenue levels (and we'll talk more about when to do that in the rest of the book), but for starters, you can do a quick inventory of your team:

How many would you say are Georges? How many are Jacks? What are you? Is your team well-balanced, or is it all-George or all-Jack?

3: Get a Coach

Getting a mentor or a business coach is something most of us fight. I get it. Well, I *used* to get it. Now, I'd say to get a mentor or coach *as soon as you can afford one.* To start with, you can use free or inexpensive resources like books, podcasts, and other content to fill your blind spots. But there's really nothing like having a trustworthy mentor that you see on a regular basis.

Those are just a few of the ways to add more Jack or George to your business. Don't worry, though—with the rest of this book, you'll find much more of what you need from the other side of the brain!

This chapter was mostly a "mindset shift" chapter. The rest of the book is *so* tactical, that I had to point out, first, that there's an overall mindset shift you need to make—you've got to realize that you have gaps in your thinking. Blind spots in the way you approach your business. Once you see your gaps, you can't unsee them.

How My Dad & I Worked Together

There's nothing wrong with being a salesman Jack or a perfectionist George,.. so long as you realize you can't do it all by yourself. By the end of this book, you'll have what you need to fulfill both roles. Even if you already have a partner that balances out your strengths, like I did with my dad, you'll be able to understand their motives that much more. Not only that, but you'll also see how essential (even if at some point, maddening) their personality is. You may not always see eye to eye, but that's the whole point: If you could scale and replicate your company all by yourself, you wouldn't be reading this book.

If you couldn't tell from my impulsive nineteen-year-old decision to take on $60,000 of work with a seven-person crew within a twenty-four-hour window, I am a certified Jack! My dad, on the other hand, was undeniably a George. With $60,000 in total revenue from those five losses, we knew we'd found something great. We combined my Jack-drive with his George-know-how and got to work, and it helped Romexterra become Chicagoland's premier restoration company.

I want the same for you.

From here on out, it's all tactics. So, get ready, because in the very next chapter, we'll be unveiling the Restoration Millionaire Method™. With it, I'm going to show you how the biggest players in the industry make millions, repeatedly. You'll find how you can quickly make your next million, too, whether it's your *first* million dollars in restoration, or you're already making $10 million+.

Let's go get that next million!

Momentum Trigger

Let's find out if you're more of a Jack or a George:

I have a simple "test" for you online at RestorationMillionaire.com/Resources that will help you identify gaps in your thinking so you can develop a full restoration business brain. Go check it out!

Restorer's Recap

- There are two types of people in almost every business—Jacks and Georges. Jacks are often salespeople or "visionaries," while Georges are typically listeners or "operators." Every restoration business needs both brains at work.
- Generally, as the leader of your company, your goal is to find out which you lean toward—either Jack or George – then ensure you develop the other part of your brain. You can do this through personal development (such as reading books or having a coach mentor you), and you can also balance your company's thinking by ensuring you have both Jacks and Georges on your team.

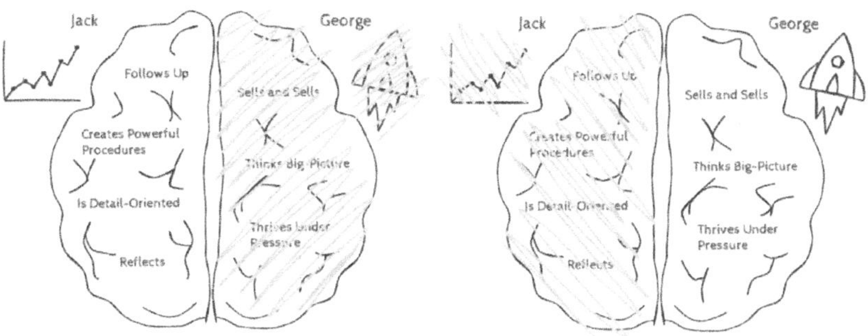

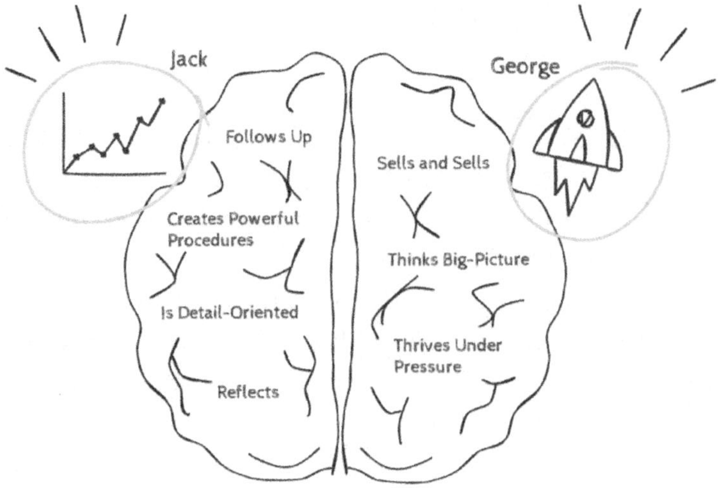

• If you're a Jack, you're probably great at sales, but poor at follow-up and collecting money. So, try to put procedures in place that help you follow-up with customers, insurance companies, and employees. You'll need playbooks and checklists to help you remember everything you need to do (we'll go into all this as the book progresses!).

• If you're a George, I bet you have plenty of amazing procedures in place. You probably pay on time, every time, and your whole team smiles when they come to work. But the problem is, often, you aren't generating many new sales, and your company is growing slowly (if at all). You need to develop your sales acumen and realize that sales is the critical component to growth in your business (you'll *love* the next chapter, which goes into this topic!).

CHAPTER 3:
The Restoration Millionaire Method™

Fishing Hole I: 1 Service & Online Marketing, $0-1 Million

New Tool

In this chapter, we're going to talk about the Restoration Millionaire Method™.

I've wrapped up the entire concept in "Fishing Holes." Basically, you start with Fishing Hole I, online marketing, and expand from there. We'll dive into the details, but here's what it looks like:

Fishing Hole I: 1 Service & Online Marketing, $0-1 Million
Fishing Hole II: Add 1 Referral Source, $1-3 Million
Fishing Hole III: Add ALL Referral Sources, $3-5 Million
Fishing Hole IV: Add New Services, $5-8 Million
Fishing Hole V: Start New Location, at Fishing Hole I

In the last chapter, I told you how my father and I got into restoration (literally, overnight!) because of a lead-generation company we'd found online.

It probably goes without saying that as soon as we found this new lead-generation source, we dove into it headfirst,.. because it was working. After that first move into online marketing, I kept going. Honestly, I wouldn't even say I "doubled down." I'd say I *quadrupled* down on online marketing.

Believing in the insane value of this new strategy, I wanted to find the absolute best online (or "digital") marketing partners in the world, so I went through what seemed like every single marketing company I could find. While many of them were slightly helpful, I kept investing and reinvesting, determined to find the absolute best marketers for Romexterra. With each new marketing company, we'd add a little more revenue, because they were typically a little bit better than the last.

On about our tenth marketing company, we found one we were really, really happy with—these guys delivered fantastic results. And the more we put into each campaign, the more leads and more revenue we would make. So, eventually, Romexterra was running $10,000 a month through them, which would earn us around $80,000 to $100,000 worth of work, all in less than eighteen months of our company starting! That was quite the turnaround for a company that was almost out of business.

"Fishing Holes"

Now, you *might* think that story is about the power of online marketing, but not exactly. What it's really about is the power of focusing on one area at a time to grow your business, the one that's driving the most impact. You see, what if we kept showing up to houses in the middle of the night, trying to avoid fist fights with the other ambulance-chasers? Obviously, we didn't bother with that after our first big win from Spark87, the digital marketing company that gave us the original leads.

Alright, let's put a pause in all the marketing talk, and let's talk about *fishing.*

If you have ever been fishing with someone who just *loves* fishing—maybe your grandpa, your aunt or uncle, or your best friend—you've probably noticed that most fishers have their favorite pond, lake, or river. In fact, most of them have their favorite *spot* at their favorite pond, lake, or river. Fishers are very, very particular, because fishing is difficult, and once you've found what works, you want to catch all the fish you can.

In fact, you can even take this to a higher level with commercial fishers; once they find a spot with big-money catches, they'll often go back to it day after day until they've caught as much as possible. Commercial fishing is expensive and uses tons of resources (crews, fuel, etc.). So, when they've found an area, they'll return again and again, until they've mined all the money they can.

This all probably sounds pretty obvious to you, but for some reason, in restoration, we often toss our nets wide, catch some, then toss them out again, to a new area, without ever pausing to ask ourselves, *Where is all the money really coming from?*

Smart restorers *do* ask that question, and then they follow it up with action—they use their resources where they're *most likely* to get more work. They focus there, until they've mastered that "Fishing Hole." Then, once they know how that hole works, they put it on auto-pilot, and move to a new hole, over and over again, utilizing each hole again and again, until they've maximized each one, systemized it, and built a fantastic business.

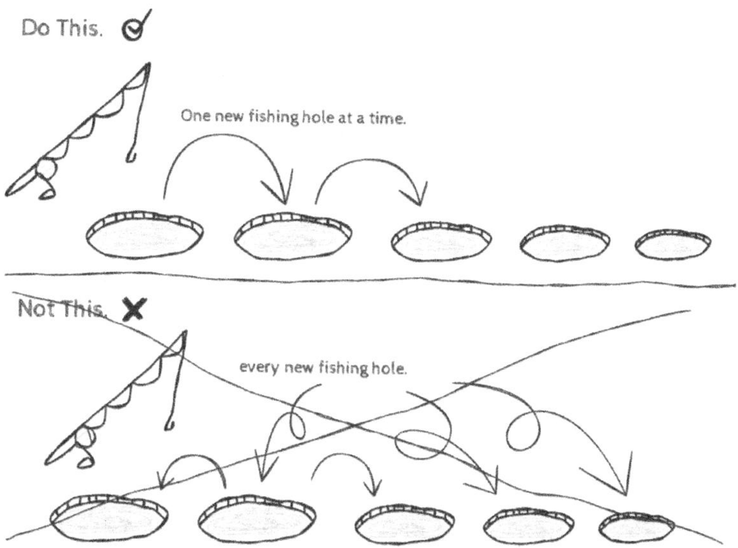

The good news is, in life, the "fish" don't really dry up. They're still there. So, when it's time "move to a new Fishing Hole," you aren't stopping fishing from one, you're just *adding* another.

Focus on One Fishing Hole at a Time

Let me paint a picture I've seen a thousand times:

Tom's a restorer who gets a little business from insurance referrals, a little bit of work from word-of-mouth, a little from other tradespeople who push business to him, and he also dabbles a little bit with social media ads. He isn't making a ton of money, and he doesn't really have a "strategy" to get more. He just says "yes" to every job and "yes" to every new marketing idea that pops into his head. Ask Tom what his company does, and he'll probably say "everything": roofing, rebuilds, reconstruction, mitigation, emergency services... you name it.

But is dividing his attention *really* the best idea? He would do far better by focusing on an area, completely dominating it, then moving onto the next, like the fishermen.

Tom the Restorer, by telling everyone he does everything, is dividing his time and attention. But what he needs to do is *focus* that time and attention. Tom should stop and ask himself:

Where is most of my money coming from? Is it coming from referrals? Is it coming from water mitigation? From rebuilds? From digital marketing? Where is the ***one place*** *I should be focusing my attention?*

If you've ever been to Texas, you've probably noticed the oil rigs going up and down, up and down. Now, oil drilling is *expensive,* easily costing well into the millions just during the initial drilling phase. Now, how silly would it be for an oil company to finally strike a deep well of oil, and then only extract a small portion of it? Of course they don't do that. Once they've done all that drilling work, and spent all those original resources, oil companies keep pulling oil out for as long as they can.

What many of us restorers do is leave tons of oil in a very, very full well. We run from one hole to the next, pumping out a little bit of oil, then moving to the next one. That goes for every area, from how we market our companies, to how we spend our time, energy, and resources, to what kind of work we do.

We need to learn to *focus.*

And that's what we're going to talk about in this chapter. I'm going to show you The Restoration Millionaire Method™, a method of focusing on *one Fishing Hole* at a time, until you've gotten all the fish you can catch, and you've hit the point where you're ready to add a new Fishing Hole. The Restoration Millionaire Method™ will offer you a systematic way to help you make your first million in revenue, quickly, if you haven't already. Then, you'll learn how to scale up to $5 million with ease. From there, you'll learn how to go to $5 million+.

Even if you have a $20 million restoration company, you'll want to use the Restoration Millionaire Method™, to ensure you are *maximizing each Fishing Hole,* to ensure you are *not leaving* business on the table, or "oil in the well." I can almost guarantee, from the data we have at Albi, that most restoration companies are leaving literally millions on the table in areas they've already started drilling, but just haven't tapped completely.

Let's get to work and find that oil and catch those fish.

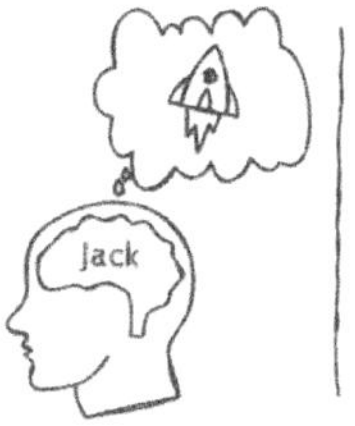

Jacks, this is especially important for you. I know you've probably been fishing from a lot of different holes, so I really need you to listen up here. Trust me. This will make your life and your business so much better. So you can get back to doing what you do best in your business.

The 4 Ways Restorers Get Work

Let's think of how restorers typically get work—often, we sign up with TPAs[8], or to be a "preferred partner" or something like that with a Big Insurance company. Then, we submit some credentials to verify we're a real company, and then, they call us when work needs to get done for one of their policyholders.

Another way is through referrals (like property managers) or work from other tradespeople (often plumbers)—maybe a buddy gets called for a job he can't complete, so he calls you for help, or just gives you the entire job. Once, I got a call from a Romanian friend of mine who was an engineer for the Chicagoland Housing Authority complex. The entire eight-story building was subsidized housing for Chicagoland seniors. One of them accidentally caught a trash bag on fire, then ran down the hallway and threw it down the trash shoot,.. and the smoke set off the sprinklers, and every, single, floor was flooded.

My buddy called me to come over right away. I signed the job, and it was one of the largest emergency service jobs we'd ever done—right about three-quarters of a million dollars in work.

Well, while I had the employees, I *didn't* have the huge semi-trucks with desiccants and generators available. For that, I called *another* friend who rolled up like the PAW Patrol with his huge vehicles, made us shine, and we paid him a huge fee.

That's pretty typical in the restoration world—from the guy who first called me, to my good friend that I called to split some of the work with; a lot of mitigation, emergency service, and frankly, trade work in general, is shared.

So, referrals are one, huge way you could get work. There are also of course relationships with homeowners, radio ads, online marketing,

---

[8] Third-party administrators, who usually work as subcontracting organizational authorities for the insurance companies.

word-of-mouth... a whole slew of potential places to find work, or, what we're calling, Fishing Holes.

Of course, you can also get work by expanding your territory or offering new services; maybe you extend the borders of your company, open a new location, or begin offering a service you didn't previously offer.

When you break all these elements down, I say there are four main ways to add new work:

Online: You can use online marketing, which is basically a systematic process that pushes people to you.

Expansion: Restores can always expand their reach by going more and more miles away from their headquarters or by simply starting a new branch in a new city or part of the city.

New services: You could provide more services to your customers.

Referrals: Restorers usually get a significant amount of their work from referrals, which usually come from plumbers, property managers, other restorers, third-party administrators or TPAs, insurance agents, other tradespeople, or other word-of-mouth offerings.

Those are the four essential ways you can add business.[9] A typical $5 million+ restoration company will probably have some mixture of the above. I want *you* to be crystal clear on where your next step is. So, in the rest of this book, we're going to learn the Restoration Millionaire Method™, which is to start with *one* Fishing Hole, then move to another one, once you've maximized it. You may be at $10 million in revenue, $500,000, or just starting out. I find, typically, it's best to start at Fishing Hole I, just to ensure you're *maximizing* each Fishing Hole.

Here's the plan that I've laid out. Now, this plan comes from talking with *hundreds,* if not thousands of other successful restorers. I have my own experience, their experiences, and tons of data and research from

---

[9] There are others, like commercials, but those are much rarer.

Albi; all of that has contributed to the following plan. So, are you ready? Here's the Restoration Millionaire Method™:

- Fishing Hole I: 1 Service & Online Marketing, $0-1 Million
- Fishing Hole II: Add 1 Referral Source, $1-3 Million
- Fishing Hole III: Add ALL Referral Sources, $3-5 Million
- Fishing Hole IV: Add New Services, $5-8 Million
- Fishing Hole V: Start New Location, at Fishing Hole I

At each Fishing Hole, you're continuing to do everything in the previous Fishing Holes, you're just adding something new.

In the rest of the book, we'll be discussing each Fishing Hole with precision, and telling you exactly how to move from one to the other, but remember – the *very first lesson,* is that you should focus on one hole at a time.

Notice that I suggest staying with only *one* service all the way until you get to Fishing Hole IV, at $5 million in revenue. Does that sound crazy to you? I get that—but remember: in restoration, you can scale up, quickly. And you'll actually be able to do that easier and faster if you focus all your efforts on one service until you're ready to branch out. Later, in chapter fifteen, we'll talk about how to tack on more services, and honestly, at that point, after going through the other Fishing Holes it's *so easy;* when my team at Romexterra added on roofing, we pulled in seven figures the first year. How? Because we already understood online marketing. We already had a referral program. We just told our prior fishing holes, "Hey, we do roofing now."

Here's what most rookies do: they put their hands into every Fishing Hole, at once, just like the newbie who's trying fishing. But what do the *experts* do? They find *one* Fishing Hole that they love, and they keep coming back for more.

I know you're thinking, *I want to go in a bunch of directions! Shouldn't I offer more than one service at a time?!* And you probably have a hundred other questions. But hang on—my goal is to help you maximize each hole. And again, even if you're above $8 million, trust me, this book is definitely still for you—in fact, you may get *more* out of it, because, you'll simply have to tighten the screws at each Fishing Hole; likely, you already have a referral program, but I'll show you how to maximize it and systemize it with CIRCLS. Maybe you already have a great company, but I'm going to give you an organizational chart that will take loads of stress off you. Regardless of how big your company is, trust me, keep reading if you're in restoration!

I can guarantee that unless you've found the point of diminishing returns (which we'll talk about later!), your *best* bet is to start with Fishing Hole I, online marketing. That means, whether you're just starting out, or you already have an eight-figure restoration company, I always tell my restoration coaching clients the same thing:

"You should probably start by taking a big look at your online marketing. Likely, you're leaving a million dollars or more on the table."

Fishing Hole I: 1 Service & Online Marketing

I follow Gary Vaynerchuk, an American-Belarusian businessman who's also from an ex-Communist country. He isn't in restoration, but he does own a zillion other companies, and here's what he says about online marketing: "There has never been a better time in the history of time, than right now to start a business."

Why was he saying that? Because of the phone in your hand. It's *so* easy now to set up online marketing, use retargeted ads, and begin to make money, quickly, for very, very little expense. And *you* don't even have to know how it all works. You can find an online marketing partner who does, and just pay them.

Here are a few other reasons you should start with online marketing:

1) Online marketing is one of the easiest marketing paths to start with, because you can do it with a computer and literally no

marketing expertise: plenty of companies will help you get started with Bing or Google Ads for a small percentage on top of your budget for the ads themselves. That's *so much easier* than trying to build out a complex referral program.

2) Another reason it's great to start with online marketing—everything is tracked on a platform. With referral marketing, word-of-mouth, or really another type of marketing, finding out how well your marketing dollars are doing in other areas is very difficult. In other words, it's *very* easy to track your costs with online marketing. Once you understand more about marketing, you can take the metrics from here, and move into the next Fishing Hole. Even if you're a $5 million company, if you're struggling with systemization, starting with online marketing will help you quickly get a handle on your marketing budget, and how to direct future marketing dollars into other areas.

3) With online marketing, you can learn how general marketing works, with very little risk. You can buy some digital ads and place them on Google or Bing, and if you (or your third-party marketing company) goofs up by putting the wrong image on an ad, spelling a word incorrectly, or messing up the link to your website, it's easy and quick to fix without too much expense.

Unless you're SERVPRO or another of the giant restoration nationals, I can nearly guarantee that online marketing is your best bet to start with, unless you're *positive* you've maxed out your ROI in this Fishing Hole.

How You Know if the Fish Are Biting

So, how do you start? Well, you start with an investment into online marketing—I'd say about $15,000 over three months. Go into it knowing that your first couple months with online marketing, you may not make a ton of additional revenue, but that's OK. After month one or two, if you've chosen a good marketing partner, you should start seeing awesome results flow in.

Now, what kind of results should you expect on those marketing dollars? In other words, how many fish should bite for that $15,000? Well, with real fishing, it's pretty easy to tell whether the fish are biting. Is your bobber going up and down? Does your pole have tension in it?

But when we talk about using online marketing, or really, any type of marketing, it's a little more complex to find out whether or not your marketing is really working. IN other words, how many fish should bite for your initial investment?

To answer that, you're going to need to learn about something called CAC, or customer acquisition cost. This is one term, even though it sounds fancy, that you probably do want to know:

CAC means what you're spending to get a new job. It's that simple.

Here's an example: So, earlier, I talked about how a marketing partner, Spark87, cost me $500 per estimate. Let's say that it took me three estimates to land a job, which would mean I had to pay Spark87 $1,500 for every new job (3 X $500 = $1,500). That means that my CAC from Spark87-related work was $1,500.

Again, CAC is simply how much money you're spending, on average, for each new job that came from your marketing. So, you could express it in real dollars, as in the example above, but usually, when you're talking about CAC, you want a *percentage*. And you find that percentage by dividing your total marketing budget by what that budget is bringing in. So, let's say that, in total, you're spending $20,000 a month on marketing, and that budget is generating $100,000 a month in work. In that case, your CAC would be 20 percent.

CAC = Marketing Budget ÷ New Work From Marketing

CAC is a very useful thing to know, even though it sounds like some fancy jargon someone made up. It tells you what percentage of each job you spent to land that job. Obviously, the lower you can get that CAC percentage while increasing your revenue, the better. But the point is you want to actually increase your revenue. When you first start your company, you may have a 0 percent CAC, because you're not spending any money on marketing. That's great, but at some point, you will absolutely need to shell out some dollars to make more. And that's what I'm suggesting here—be willing to spend a *percentage* of your job costs on acquiring that job.

Overall, most restorers should shoot for a CAC around 10-20.

Again, just remember: Your CAC will probably shoot through the roof for a couple months when you first dive into a new Fishing Hole or start with a new online marketing partner. But, over time, it should level out to 20 percent or less.

What the CAC?

I know—why am I bringing up this odd term? Well, it's *super* important to us in business, but you definitely shouldn't feel weird if you haven't heard of it before.

My team recently spoke with the incredible Ricelli Mordecai, who's in a fractional role helping restoration company owners (and others) maximize profits and gain stronger footholds with their marketing and/or sales campaigns. So, she knows a ton of fancy terminology and she's a beast at explaining it well. She shared a wild story of another restoration-business owner who'd found, at some level, massive success. Here's what she said about their conversation:

> *I talked to a founder a couple days ago, whose restoration company had brought in $15 million last year. I asked him for his COGs[1], and he said, "What's that?" so I explained the term. Then I asked, "What's your cost of customer acquisition, or CCA?"[1] same reply. After a few more questions with similar responses, he finally said, "My goodness. I feel silly."*

No reason he should have felt silly—nor should you. In any other field, you don't make it to eight figures without knowing about COGs, CAC, EBITDA (next chapter!), or how to read a profit-and-loss statement. But in restoration, by hard work and hustle, it's possible for someone like me or you to come from nothing, then arrive at millions in revenue.

So, in this book, I'm going to *only* give you the terms you really need, with the easiest explanations possible. CAC is one of those terms!

4 Tips on Online Marketing

I have a few tips for those starting out with online marketing:

- **Start with about $3,000 to $5,000 per month.** If you start with less than that, your results will be skewed. (If you don't have that much to spend on digital marketing, DIY it—build your own Google or Bing Ads and run the campaigns yourself.)

- **Use a third-party marketer who specializes in restoration.** Assuming you have at least $5,000 a month to spend on marketing, use a third-party marketer who will be able to drive results faster. I suggest one that specializes in digital marketing for restoration or at least the trades. (Easy hack: just google "digital marketing for restoration company" and you'll find plenty of options very quickly.)

- **Find three options.** To find the best third-party marketer, narrow down your third-party options to three, then get on a call with all of them and ask these questions:

    1) *How many leads can you deliver for $5,000 per month?*

    2) *What platform do you use to allow me to see how my ads are performing?*

- **Give it three months.** Once you pick a third-party marketer (or decide to DIY it), then stick to a general plan for two to three months. It takes a couple months and a few tries to get the marketing right, so if you switch strategies too quickly, you won't see any results. If you still aren't seeing plenty of new leads after three months, change your strategy, and change out your third-party marketer if you have one.

A Marketing Snowball

When you double-down on online marketing, you can easily get to a $1 million directly from those online ads, not including what you're making from word-of-mouth or other sources. That's why online marketing should typically be your first Fishing Hole.

And here's the insane thing: Once you get *one* Fishing Hole down, each one becomes easier and easier, because you've already made a name and reputation for yourself and really done a fantastic job in one area. So, let's say you take my advice (and you should!) and start with online marketing. After you've hit around a $1 million in revenue, you'll have a ton of customer reviews, been into a thousand customer homes, and have tons of employees. Now, it will be *so much easier* to implement Fishing Hole II: Add 1 Referral Source.

If you really focus on doing well in one Fishing Hole before moving on to the next, you'll pick up more and more momentum as you move along, like a snowball.

Georges. You may be tempted to stay in a Fishing Hole, especially if it's been working for you. But once you've maximized one Fishing Hole, you need to keep moving. Read on to find out how; trust me! You want to keep growing.

Momentum Trigger

This chapter, I have two options for your Momentum Trigger, depending on whether you've used online marketing or you haven't:

If you have no online marketing:

1) Go online and research online marketers who specialize in marketing for restoration, or at least the trades.

2) Narrow your list down to three and make appointments with each one.

3) Ask these questions during your interview with each:

"How many leads can you deliver for $5,000 per month?"

"What platform do you use to allow me to see how my ads are performing?"

4) Start by investing $3,000 to $5,000 a month and give it ninety days. If by the end of that ninety days, you aren't seeing at least $25,000 a month in new work, try another online marketer.

If you *do* use online marketing, but aren't sure if you've maxed out your returns yet:

1) Determine your CAC (customer acquisition cost). Simply divide what you're spending on online marketing by what work that budget is bringing in. So, if you're spending $20,000 and bringing in $150,000 worth of work, you'd divide the budget by the work and get roughly 13 percent.

2) See how much more you can increase your online budget without shifting too far from that CAC.

3) Keep going until you hit the point of diminishing returns; once you do, go on to the next piece of homework here:

Once you max out the online marketing Fishing Hole, you're ready for your next Fishing Hole! Check out chapter nine!

Restorer's Recap

- Struggling restorers travel halfway down a dozen different paths to find new business—they expand their territory too far, they try to make partners out of every other trade industry, they dabble in online marketing, and the list goes on. *Eight- and nine-figure restoration companies* do the opposite: They start with one pathway to finding new business. Once they've mastered one marketing area, they systemize it and move onto a new method of marketing, all while maintaining the prior method. Using this method, each new method of marketing becomes easier. In this chapter, we called these new pathways to business "Fishing Holes."
- The best Fishing Hole for restorers to start mastering first is online marketing.

- The Restoration Millionaire Method™ is a step-by-step process that we'll go through in the rest of the book:
    - Fishing Hole I: 1 Service & Online Marketing, $0-1 Million
    - Fishing Hole II: Add 1 Referral Source, $1-3 Million
    - Fishing Hole III: Add ALL Referral Sources, $3-5 Million
    - Fishing Hole IV: Add New Services, $5-8 Million
    - Fishing Hole V: Start New Location, at Fishing Hole I[10]

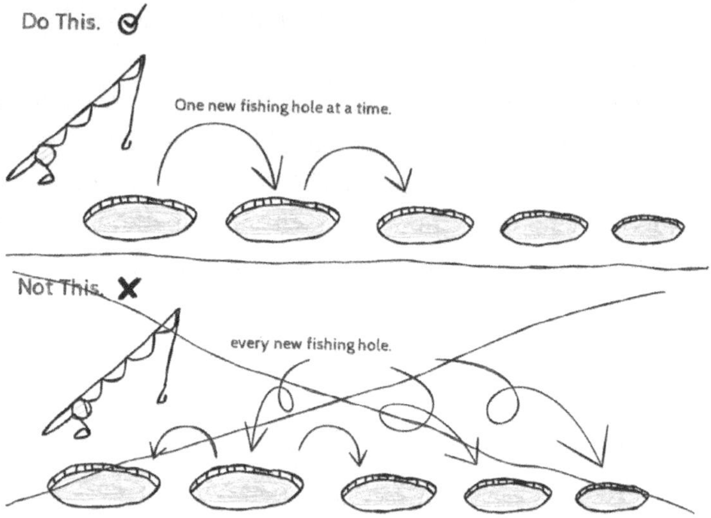

- Most restorers, even if they have millions in revenue, should start by using the Restoration Millionaire Method™, to ensure they've maximized and systemized each Fishing Hole before moving on.

---

[10] For Fishing Holes II and III, go to chapter nine. For Fishing Holes IV and V, go to chapter fifteen.

CHAPTER 4:
The 48-Hour Rule™

"Watch your money. It'll land on your feet."
—Del Paxton in That Thing You Do

New Tool

In this chapter, we're going to go over the 48-Hour Rule™:

Follow-up with every invoice every 48 business hours until it's paid.

If you follow this simple rule, you'll almost always be paid within thirty days.

I'd like to paint a picture of how bills are usually sent and paid in the restoration industry. If you're new to this field, or just considering jumping into it, this quick example may give you an idea of how the whole system works, but don't worry. In the rest of the chapter, I'll give you a *very* easy way to cash-in and avoid much of the pain that you're going to read about in a moment! While this story is technically fictional, it's the sort I've heard (and been a part of!) *hundreds* of times.

Jimmy's the owner of a small restoration company. He's just about to finish a giant job on a home after a bad flood swept through the neighborhood. Jimmy managed the work himself and used a couple subcontractors to help out.

After drying the home and removing any excess water, Jimmy asks Mrs. Homeowner to sign his completion of work, which she does and says, "Thank you."

Now, Jimmy has another job to rush off to...

About a week later, the two subcontractors he used for that big water-mitigation job start asking for their money. Also, Jimmy needs to buy a couple thousand-dollars-worth of tools from Home Depot for the *new* job he's just landed. Lastly, he also needs subcontractors for this new, big job, but he feels a little embarrassed to ask the two he worked with previously until he's paid them what he owes them.

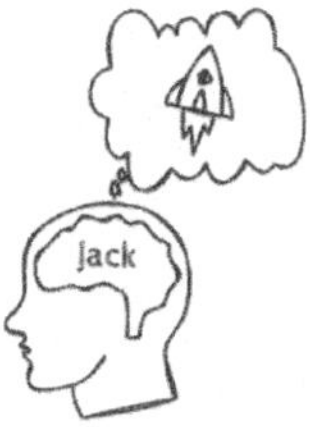

Jacks, does this story sound familiar?

Jimmy checks out his business bank account to see what he has available. *I'm getting low,* he thinks. But, luckily, the insurance company for Mrs. Homeowner owes him plenty of money. *I'll just send over my invoice to the insurance adjuster. That should handle it.* Jimmy hops on his laptop and puts together his invoice then fires it off to the insurance adjuster; by now, it's been ten days since he finished the work.

A week goes by, and he doesn't hear anything from the insurance adjuster. *I'll give him until Friday,* Jimmy thinks.

Still nothing. So, Jimmy sends a quick email. "Hey Mr. Adjuster! Just following up on our previous invoice!"

A couple days later, and he does hear back, but instead of a check or an approval, he gets a request to revise. By now, Jimmy's knee-deep in the new job and doesn't have time to immediately revise his invoice.

A few days later, he finally gets around to revising the invoice, and sends it back to Mr. Adjuster. It's now been over a month since the work was completed, and he really needs to pay his subcontractors. He waits a week, then calls the adjuster, who says, "Hey thanks for sending over the revised invoice, Jimmy. I'll take a look at it ASAP. It's been a long week. You know how it goes."

Another week, and Jimmy hears nothing.

He sends a follow up email, a text, and a call. By now, he's panicking. He's coming up on sixty days since he finished the job, and he hasn't even heard if the last estimate has been approved. Even once the insurance *does* approve it, he'll have to wait five to seven days until the homeowner receives the check. *Then* he'll have to go over to their house and pick it up, cash it, and wait for it to clear...

I call this the "Cashflow Nightmare*,"* and it's a recurring dream that many in restoration have every night (or day)!

On one hand, it probably feels like it's out of Jimmy's control. Sure, he could have done a better job following up and invoicing, but here's what's interesting: Collecting payments usually becomes a struggle the *better* a company is doing, because really good restorers who do quality work and care about their customers, get really busy, really quickly. Plus, restorers are usually the nice guys. They care more about getting the job done right than they do about getting paid. So, as they get busier and busier, staying on top of the sometimes pain-in-the-neck adjusters (who are the bottleneck for most restoration payments) often falls to the wayside.

That's why I have a prediction for most new restorers (who haven't read this book!):

Without a collections gameplan, every great sales month will create a Cashflow Nightmare three months later.

So, if you are not careful, more work will just land you back on the Reactive Rollercoaster™ we talked about in Chapter 1...

The Reactive Rollercoaster

This can *really* hurt because your employees can't wait to get paid. They'll always need the money ASAP. You also may have a note on a truck or be paying a huge lease on a warehouse space, not to mention new tools you'll need and other vendors you'll need to pay, most of whom demand to get paid like clockwork, regardless of whether or not *you've* been paid. Meaning that more work can actually create *less* cashflow.

But it doesn't have to be that way—you just need a plan, and I have one for you, one that I've tested and perfected over the years. Follow this, and you'll actually be rewarded for your company's growth. It works like this: If you assume that you're going to have to do seven to fifteen touches with interested parties before you get paid, then, make sure you **follow-up with each touch every 48 hours business hours**. In the end, if you do that, most of your jobs will get paid out in thirty days.

I call this the 48-Hour Rule: Follow up with every invoice every 48 business hours.

The exception to this is the *first* time you send an invoice to the adjuster or insurance company; on that initial send, after confirming receipt, you may need to give them one week to look at it. That's it. No more than a week and *confirm* that they're looking at it and going to get back to you.

So, send an invoice to the adjuster, give it 48 hours, then set a date *no more* than one week out from when it was sent, that they will get back to you. If you do this, even with all the back-and-forth, as long as you're following up every 48 hours, you should get your invoice paid inside thirty days most of the time.

If, instead, you do what Jimmy did, you'll end up with seven to ten days in between each touch. Honestly, if you're not careful, it can take ninety days *or more* to get paid that way. Plus, the *longer* you take in between follow-up, the less likely the adjusters and others are going to think they need to pay you on time. After all, it's the squeaky wheel that gets the oil.

On the other hand, though, since you'll be dealing with many of the same adjusters, insurance companies, and other contractors repeatedly, if you get them all used to the fact that **you get paid every thirty days**, everyone will just get used to the fact that they need to pay you first. Because, they know that every 48 hours, you'll be talking to them.

Don't worry—I'm not talking about being rude. I'm talking about being pleasantly persistent. There's a way to follow up with a smile on your voice, in your email, and on your face.

Solve Problems by Bringing Cash Forward

The real-life George from chapter two came to me a couple years ago to ask for some coaching. He had a small team, and he was doing about half a million in revenue. A few months into our time together he told me, "I think I need to make some payroll cuts." George's business account balance was getting dangerously low, and he was getting very, very nervous.

(Now, on one hand, way to go George, for actually *looking ahead!* Something us Jacks rarely do!)

George wanted to cut expenses. So, I asked him:

"OK, George, what expenses do you want to cut?"

"Well, let's see. Who do we have on payroll?" George asked, as he started going through the list. "We have marketing partner, our internal sales team, our production team..."

George knew he couldn't cut the subcontractors who were doing the actual work. So, naturally, he started eyeing the marketing partner and the sales team.

"OK, George, let's say we cut the marketing spend. Then what will happen in ninety days?" I asked him.

"Well, our cashflow problem will be solved today, but I bet we'll have a lot less work coming through the door in a couple months. Hmm..."

I didn't have to say anything else. George answered his own question and filled in the scenario himself:

"And if I have less work coming in, I'll eventually have to cut some of the sales team, which means I'll be able to take on less sales calls, which will mean less sales." He said.

"Yup," I said. "And what then?"

"Well, then, we'll have less sales and less cash..."

George's eyes started getting big, as he imagined his company shriveling.

"Don't worry, George," I said, realizing I might have been a little hard on him. "What about these accounts receivables? What if we just pulled some of that forward? How much do people owe you?"

"About $150,000 that hasn't been paid yet."

"Wow! That's great. What would an extra $150,000 do to your bank account?"

"Well, that would solve all my cashflow problems," George offered.

That may seem obvious to you when you're reading the story, but when you're in the middle of a business fight, you typically think of only two levers when it comes to cashflow—getting more jobs or cutting costs. But the hidden lever, the one everyone forgets about, is collecting cash you're already owed.

> It's much less expensive to collect money that people already owe you than it is to get new work.

If people owe you money, then most of the time, almost all of it, is pure profit—you've probably already paid out some of your subcontractors (or all of them), paid some of the commissions, and likely all of the marketing costs, and you've probably already paid for the materials. What's left over is almost all yours!

Let's take a real example—say that your typical profit margin is 20 percent, and you have $100,000 outstanding that customers still owe you. To get an additional $100,000 in cash, you could:

A) Cut out expenses, which will probably slow your company's growth

B) Go land *$500,000* worth of new work, which could get you $100,000 of extra cash, at 20 percent profit

C) Simply go collect that $100,000 that you're owed

I mean, which of the above sounds easier?

Option C? I think so, too!

When More Money = Less Cash

I don't blame George for the cashflow issue. This doesn't just happen to Georges. It happens to plenty of Jacks, too. In fact, I think it happens to Jacks *more* often, because they get so caught up with all the new work they have.

Our second year in the restoration business, my father and I were making $3 million in revenue. That was *so* cool as a nineteen-year-old! And that's by *no* means odd—we bootstrapped the whole company, and many restorers do the same, and quickly find themselves in seven or more figures in revenue.

But, also like other restorers, we started running into cashflow problems. In fact, no matter how many more jobs we landed, Romexterra's bank account never seemed to be very full. My father was getting concerned.

"We're making three times what we made our first year, but the bank account looks no different; Why are we trying to grow the company so much if we aren't making any more money?"

Well, we *were* making more money, but Alex wasn't doing a good job of collecting it.

If you want to become your own Restoration Millionaire, and do it quickly, you've simply got to pay attention to your cashflow. Don't end up like we did for a while, making three times the money with nothing to show for it. I learned the following lesson the hard way, but you don't have to. So, here's how make sure *you* always get paid in thirty days:

The four cash-collection rules of a Restoration Millionaire:

1) Call Your Shot
2) Be Pleasantly Persistent
3) Use Multi-touch With All Interested Parties
4) Observe the "48-Hour Rule™"

1: Call Your Shot

From the very beginning, you need to *call your shot* with your homeowners.

Let every person know, from day one, and repeatedly after that:

"We get paid in thirty days."

In fact, just say that to yourself. Go ahead, seriously, say it out loud. There's something powerful about saying it definitively like that, even to yourself. Don't say, "We *try* to get paid in thirty days," or "We *hope* to get paid in thirty days." Practice saying, repeatedly, simply:

"We get paid in thirty days."

And you can pair it with another definitive statement, "We do the highest-quality work, and we get paid in thirty days." Again, this isn't about "trying." It's about doing. As Yoda said: "Do or do not. There is no try."

By planting a stake in the ground from day one, your customers won't be surprised down the road.

Georges, this will be a game changer for you. You thrive on systems, and it probably feels like your systems aren't working super well. Try this. It may feel a bit weird at first, but I think you'll love the results.

2: Be Pleasantly Persistent

Secondly, you've got to be pleasantly persistent. Again, you want to be a squeaky wheel that demands oil (or payment) but not so squeaky that you're annoying. Along the process, you want to let the homeowner, the adjuster, and anyone else involved know, "I'm sure you'll have no problem ensuring we get paid in thirty days. We've really enjoyed working together!" Basically, just keep calling your shot, being persistent about it, but saying it with a smile in your voice, or a smiley in your email.

3: Use Multi-Touch With All Interested Parties

At Romexterra, we don't just send an email, a text, or drop a phone call. We do all three. And we do it with everyone involved with payment.

In restoration, most of our business goes through the insurance adjuster—we send our invoices to them for approval. At Romexterra, because we've brought the homeowner in on the process, when it's time to send in the bill, we CC them on everything, and we do it every way possible. (I say "we," but now, it's really my father! I went to start Albi!)

When it's time to send your invoice, email the adjuster, CC-ing the homeowner. Then, text the adjuster and the homeowner. Then, *call* the adjuster, and the customer: "Hey! We just sent out the first invoice for your work. I'm sure it'll get taken care of quickly."

4: Observe the 48-Hour Rule™

Never go more than 48 business hours without following up with an adjuster. The only exception is the *first,* original estimate, in which case you can give them up to a week (and no more) to review it.

This 48-Hour Rule™ should start the minute a project gets wrapped up.

Each of our project managers at Romexterra has two business days from the time the job is completed to send out the initial invoice to all parties. Then, from there, every two business days, they know that there should be some sort of activity happening with it until it's paid.

So, if we finish a job on Friday, the invoice should be sent by Tuesday at the latest. By Thursday, you should be following up with the adjuster:

"Hey Adjuster, did you have a chance to look at the invoice? No? That's OK? *When* will you have a chance to look at it? Actually, no, two weeks is not acceptable. Let's say next Tuesday. I'll call you back at 11 a.m. to verify, OK?"

Then, on the following Tuesday, time to call. Then, call again on Thursday, then again on Monday. Along the way, you should be saying this to the homeowner:

"Hey Mr. Homeowner! I sent the invoice today, and the adjuster and I are talking *next* Thursday about it, just to make sure it's approved, and *we always get paid within thirty days.*"

Some restorers think following up every two days is just too much. I get that, but think about how many phases most invoices have to go through: There's an invoice, then a revision phase, then an approval, then a check gets cut, and then you have to go pick it up from the customer's house. That's if there are *no* hiccups along the way, and, often, there's a lot of back-and-forth during that revisions phase.

Overall, I'd say most jobs need seven to fifteen touches (per party). So, if you follow up within two days at every touch and it takes you ten touches total, you'll get paid inside a month (with weekends). If instead, you only followed up once every *seven days,* it could easily take you two or three months to get paid.

Set Expectations From the Get-Go

Part of calling your shot up front means you also let the homeowner in on your process, including what would happen if you were not paid on time. Let the homeowner know the truth – that you're more or less extending them a loan to get started on the work, and that you'll do your best to get the insurance company to pay, but it's ultimately the homeowner's job.

Some restorers never tell the homeowners the truth, that they are ultimately responsible for the payment. Instead, some just try to take the easy way out and say, "Don't worry about it. We'll get all the money from your insurance company."

I don't think that's the easy way. I'd say that's the *lazy* way. If you sell with the "don't worry your insurance will pay" line, then, if and when there *is* a problem with the insurance company, and you need the homeowner's help to talk with the insurance company, how is that going to work? Your customer is going to feel lied to.

Instead, when you let your customer know your process (and the consequences) up front, they join *your* team, and now, if there's a problem, it becomes Mrs. Homeowner + Restorer vs. Insurance Company.

So, call your shot early, letting the homeowner in on your process -– "We get paid in thirty days." You were there with them when their home got flooded or there was a fire; now, they should be there for you when it's time to get paid.

Next, remain pleasantly persistent throughout the process. Be firm but do it with a "smile" in your voice. Use multi-touch with all interested parties—send an email, write a text, *and* a call. And CC everyone.

Finally, no matter what, follow the 48-Hour Rule™: never let more than 48 business hours go by without following up on an invoice.

Do all this, and, even with an adjuster who asks for a revision, then wants to negotiate, you'll end up with about seven to fifteen touches, multiplied by two days, and you'll *still* get paid in under thirty days.

About to Stall? Add Power

Having cash in the bank is what allows you to make good decisions, frequently. Remember George, at the beginning of the chapter? He was a smart guy, and he was about to *cut* his marketing team to save money, which would have probably tanked his company in the long run. Luckily, he reached out to me for help before he did anything rash.

I'm a certified Jack, who got far too caught up in selling that I never paused to think about how to collect all the money we were making. Luckily, I had my father around, and he and I kept each other from making silly mistakes. But a lot of restorers aren't as fortunate as George or I am: Faced with a cashflow problem, many business owners do exactly what George was about to do—they cut costs (usually payroll), which solves the temporary cashflow issue. But then, about three months later, they have an even bigger problem to deal with—a shrinking company.

Interestingly, when you're faced with a cashflow problem, you typically have to act *counter-punitively.* You can't do the seemingly natural thing and pull the brakes, or otherwise, you'll destroy your business. It's kind of like hitting a stall in an airplane. I've had the privilege of learning how to fly over the last few years, and one of the things they teach you during pilot training is how to get out of a stall.

A stall can happen anytime, but one of the scariest and most common is when you're coming in to land. Now, the natural thing to do when you start to stall during a landing is to simply pull up, away from the ground, away from the perceived danger. This seems to make sense—the plane's about to hit "zero altitude," so your gut tells you to pull up, in the opposite direction, away from the danger. But the problem is, that's *not* what you need to do.

While it feels like the problem with a stall is the ground, the real, underlying problem with a stall is the loss of speed and power. So, to solve a speed and power problem, you add speed and power—instead of pulling up, you actually point your nose slightly downward and add more juice to the engine. This creates lift, helping you recover from the stall.

Trust me—when you're flying in an airplane toward a runway with a stalled engine, adding power and speed feels awkward, because your stomach is screaming that you're heading toward altitude-zero, even quicker. But you learn to overcome this fear with practice. And that's what you have to do as a business owner facing cashflow problems. Your gut instinct may be to pull away from "altitude zero," which, in the case of finances, means zero dollars in the bank account. Instead, though, what you need to do is actually lean into the pressure and add more dollars to your bank account. And the easiest way to do that is simply by bringing cash forward.

Momentum Trigger

Today's Momentum Trigger is simple—I want you to learn how to calculate how fast you're collecting your money. Technically, this is called your "turn on receivables." I offer the math below, which will help you calculate this, but if you want a simpler way, just go to RestorationMillionaire.com/Resources, and I have a calculator for your turn on receivables there!

Turn on Receivables Calculation

There are a lot of complicated ways to calculate this, but here's the basic formula, the one that restorers should usually use:

Total Accounts receivable ÷ 90-day average monthly sales X 30

The resulting number from the above calculation tells you how long, on average, it's taking you to get paid.

If this seems a bit foreign, here's the explanation:

- Your "accounts receivable" is the amount of money you're still owed for work you already did.
- Your "90-day average monthly sales," is exactly what it sounds like – the average sales you've made every month over the last three months.
- The number "30" is a rounded number for a month. (Technically, if the year were divided up into twelve equal months, the answer would be 365/12, or about 30.416, but I say just use 30!)

Let's walk through a quick example. Say that Cherry Restoration Company currently has $150,000 in accounts receivable, and their 90-day average monthly sales is $75,000, they would have a turn on receivables of 60 days:

$150,000 / $75,000 * 30 = 60

So, to find your own turn on receivables, use the above formula, or go to RestorationMillionaire.com/Resources to use our restoration-friendly calculator.

Restorer's Recap

- Without a collections gameplan, a great sales month will create a Cashflow Nightmare three months later. The restoration industry requires that you do the work first, then get paid later. While you're waiting to get paid, you'll need to pay out for subcontractors, vendors, and tool rentals. So, the more work you bring in, the more you have to pay out, and if you aren't careful, more work will actually create a thinner bank account.
- Sometimes the kindest restorers, those who are great with customers, often have the hardest time collecting payments: They're nice, and they focus more on the work than they do on collecting payments. That's why you bring the homeowner into your process and set the exceptions *early on,* to get them on your side, in case there's an issue collecting payments with the insurance company.
- Solving the cashflow problem is simple, but you have to follow a system. Here's my simple system:
    - Call your shot with the homeowner. Make it part of your sales process. Tell the homeowner, from the very beginning, "We get paid in thirty days."
    - Be pleasantly persistent—don't let up on the adjuster, or the customer, but do it with a smile on your face.
    - Use multi-touch with all interested parties. Don't just call, or text, or email. Do all three, with the homeowners, the adjuster, and anyone else who's involved with your payments.
    - Observe the 48-Hour Rule™. If you remember only one thing, remember this: You follow the 48-Hour Rule™. Within two business days of job completion, every invoice is sent out, and consistently followed-up with every two business days until it's paid. (The only exception is in the initial review phase—it's OK to give an adjuster up to *one week* to review the initial invoice.)

- How to get paid in thirty days: 10 touches X 2 business days in between touches ≈ 30 days (with weekends).

CHAPTER 5:
Dream in 4D

New Tool

In this chapter I'm going to teach you how to dream big. Really big.

Specifically, we're going to learn about 4D Dreaming; in this model you get very, very detailed about your dreams:

The 4D Dream™ has these four elements:

- **Disneyfy it:** Whatever your first thought of your dream is, 10X it.
- **Date it:** How long is this dream going to take to accomplish? Put a real, future time on it.
- **Detail it:** What does your big dream taste, feel, and smell like it? Who's there? Where are you?
- **Draw it:** Physically write down your dream, or paint it, or put it together with magazine clippings. Get it out of your head and onto paper somehow.

Whether you're a fan of comic books, superhero movies, or historic figures, you've most likely heard the famous quote, "With great power, there must also come great responsibility." This famous line, commonly recited as a line from *Spiderman,*[11] has been used to bolster someone up when the challenge seems too great, or to sober someone up when the responsibility was too much. In this case, I'm going to do both.

When you started restoration, you probably had no idea how much responsibility you had to take on. Whether you immigrated into America and needed a job that didn't require years of experience, or just wanted to earn a fast profit, you probably used it as a way to pay the bills and support your family, as my dad and I did. And in the beginning of running a business, there's nothing wrong with that.

Take my colleague, Randy, for example. Back in the 2010s, Randy had the idea to open up a little coffee shop in Colorado Springs. Frankly, to most, it probably seemed like he just got tired of working on his computer in the nearby Starbucks, having to pay five bucks for a latte every day. Or maybe everyone thought he just assumed it would be a fun little side gig to build on his own. Regardless, at some level, Randy didn't have a ton of ideas on how to even run a coffee shop, let alone the issues he was going to deal with. I mean, his nightmare stories alone could fill a book: theft within the company, tax issues, backed up plumbing due to bad installation (yeah, he did the plumbing himself), over-the-counter fist fights, homeless drug-users using the bathrooms to "shower" in the sink … you name it, he's been through it.

Hopefully, you've never seen a fight in restoration (although I *have* actually seen fists thrown between restorers who were scrambling to land the same fire rebuild!). Yet, I do imagine you've had your share of problems to work through. Like hiring an experienced technician, all to fire him within the month because he wouldn't stop swearing in front of clients. Or, maybe landing six projects within the span of a week, but only having enough equipment to handle three of them. But, like Randy, through trial and error, occasional bad customer reviews, and mistakes

---

[11] It was also in the 1962 Spider-Man comic "Amazing Fantasy #15," and it's also been attributed to others, such as Winston Churchill and even Voltaire!

from either you or your employees, you've managed to build up your business to where it is today.

Let's revisit Randy's coffee shop again, but fast forward a decade. Between political campaigns, local car shows, weddings and receptions, televised interviews, Wednesday open-mic nights, Sunday morning brunch club, and a dozen other events held within its four walls (not to mention his kids have even found their spouses there), it's become a powerhouse of the community. In providing jobs to immigrants, ex-convicts, and recovering users, it's recognized as a life-giving hub for nearby neighborhoods. It's won local awards, yielded thousands of dollars in stable, nearly passive income for Randy (who no longer runs the shop) and has provided a job for every single one of his ten kids as they've grown up. People from across the country have heard of Randy's amazing "little coffee shop."

What's even crazier is, early on, everyone in Randy's circle told him his shop was going be a cash hog. His family got tired of the hassle and never-ending problems that come with owning a business, and on several occasions, told him to quit. But Randy had a sparkle in his eye. In his gut, he *knew* that despite all the tax issues, employee conflicts, and whatever else, his shop would become something greater than anyone could have predicted.

Now, just imagine what your "little restoration company" could become. If you have a vision for what your restoration company could really be – financially and socially – then all the problems you're going to face? The responsibility you unknowingly took on? They won't seem like that big of a deal anymore.

Look at the following scenario, for example:

It's a year from now, and your business is on track to do $5 million in revenue by the end of the year. The sales are there, you're pretty tired from the hustle, but you know that in two years, with the right people and proper focus, your company will be worth $10 million or more to a prospective buyer. You know that not only will you be able to use the money from your business to put your kids through college, but many of your employees will be able to do the same, and there will even be money left over for them to take vacations. Your business can even provide enough money to help the community pay for local sports teams, fund charities, and even send underprivileged kids to expensive theater and sports camps.

Kids, college tuition, car payments, mortgages, community fundraisers... Whatever you think is possible is just the tip of the iceberg. So, when whoever first wrote or said, "With great power, there must also come great responsibility," they weren't kidding. Wielding the power and responsibility of an entrepreneur *is* hard, but when you compare it to the real opportunity available, like how Randy saw his vision through the homeless sink-showers and backed up drainpipes, the pressure and all those responsibilities start to shrink in significance.

In this chapter, I'm going to teach you how to handle both power and responsibility with confidence and clarity. You'll have confidence in making small decisions which previously bogged down your daily checklist, and you'll maintain clarity about why you're pushing through seemingly never-ending obstacles to reach your goal.

Along the way, we'll discuss how you can use your vision to inspire a culture of dreamers, a work environment where everyone is dedicated to the end goal. Then, we'll talk about how to give back to your team and to your communities, before finally learning what it looks like to dream in 4D, four simple instructions for how to clarify your dream.

The Dream

As an entrepreneur, you've gained the ability to think on your feet. On a day-to-day basis, you probably rattle off a hundred commands to various people, all without a second thought. But getting stuck in this fix-it mode can make it difficult to slow down when big decisions that need more than five seconds of thought come up, the biggest one being the direction of your company.

If someone were to ask you, "Where will your business be in ten years?" What comes to mind? If someone asked my dad and me that question in the early days at Romexterra, we would have shrugged and said, "Make $100,000 each by the end of the year." I'm not kidding... *That was the only thing in our hearts and minds.*

When you picture the future of your company, do you have a crystal-clear picture in your head, like who's standing next to you and what amount you want sitting in the bank? Can you see what car you're driving and what house you're living in? Or does your future look and feel more like a quick sketch done by one of your technicians when he tries to explain how many air movers a confused customer needs? If you're like most restoration founders I know (like myself), you fall into the second category. You like quick, drawn-up solutions that get you moved on to the next problem fast. But to move forward, you need to have a clear idea of where you're headed, and that takes some careful planning.

So, the first step is to think of the big picture, or The Dream, and The Dream needs to be *huge*. And when I say huge, I mean so big that people will call you crazy for it.

Take Walt Disney for example. He started out as a high-school drop-out who liked to draw, and after reading a book on animation, he opened his own animation company. Shortly after, it went bankrupt, but he didn't quit. With the help of his brother, Roy, they moved to Hollywood and tried again. He had the idea to be the first animator to produce a feature-length animated film. They called him crazy, saying no one would want to watch a whole movie full of just cartoons. But because of Walt's persistence, after four years of planning, and nearly going bankrupt, in 1937, *Snow White and the Seven Dwarves* went on to win an Academy Award, paving the way for the universe of animated films we know today.[12]

Walt's vision for animating full-length films wasn't the dream; that was just the beginning. His dream wasn't even to become the most famous animator in the world, though that's what he became. His real

---

[12] Carus, David. "'They' Called Walt Disney Crazy, 'No One Would Watch a Whole Movie of a Cartoon'" David Carus, June 28, 2012.

dream was to create a world for families to disappear into the magic and wonder of his characters, and for millions of creators to follow after him and fulfill their dreams. People called him even more crazy for it, but to him, that just meant he was on the right track.

Picture what your dream could be for your life, your business, your employees, and even your community.

Big Dreams Create Energy for Today

What makes you get out of bed in the morning? For most entrepreneurs, it's the day-to-day battle. It might be your instinct to work hard no matter what's put in front of you, or maybe it's your need to do right by those working under you. Solving today's problems may be enough motivation for you, today, but eventually, without something more, you'll burn out. Think of it like this—what if you told the following to a young Michael Phelps:

"Here's an idea for the next couple decades of your life: You're going to miss your friends' birthday parties. You're going to get up very early, every day. You won't get to watch TV or eat fun foods. You'll be working harder than everyone else. You're going to be sore, with pain all over your body. You're going to get ear infections and have to wear annoying clothes..."

Picture saying *all* the above but leaving out the critical detail that Michael Phelps had the shot at being an elite-level Olympic swimmer. I don't know about you, but without that critical detail, my response would be, "Kick rocks!"

But that's what a huge dream does. It helps today's problems makes sense. It gives you a path forward, and motivation for today. If you lose that vision, you can quickly become lost. You may putter along for a while, but eventually you may ask yourself, *Why am I even doing this?*

There's an ancient Jewish proverb that goes like this, "Without a vision, people perish." The author knew that if you lose sight of the "why," you'll eventually lose your way. So, if you make that dream *huge,* you'll have enough juice to get there.

And, when you make that dream big enough, it doesn't just motivate you, but it also motivates others...

Your Dreams Fuel Others

What about your employees? Imagine what gets them out of bed in the morning: the need to pay bills, routine, pure necessity ... the same reasons for nearly all of America's working class. But what if you could make it more than that?

As we all know, our team is what makes your dream even possible. But not just any team will get you there. It takes careful hiring to retain and reward the *right* people. Whether you've struggled with employee commitment, or you can't seem to get people excited about the future, don't worry – we're going to cover exactly how to motivate your team and make the dream happen.

In April 2021, McKinsey & Company released an article entitled, "Help your employees find purpose–or watch them leave." In, it the authors explain why it's so important that employers help employees find a sense of value in their daily work, for many reasons, not the least of which is sheer productivity. Per the study: "People who live their purpose at work are more productive than people who don't. They are also healthier, more resilient, and more likely to stay at the company."

As a leader, it's your job to ensure your dream encompasses all the dreams of your employees. They must feel their purpose is not only being fulfilled in their current role, but their goals are possible through the growth within the company. And if they are not, it's your responsibility to find out why, and how to fix it. Your dreams, essentially, have to be big enough to fit *all theirs* within it. Otherwise, they won't stick around.

At your company, your employees aren't just coming to work to collect a paycheck every two weeks; they should be showing up because they have a sense of purpose in their work. They need to know, through your direct communication, that each of them is there because of what they bring to the table, and what they'll get in return. No randomness, no stroke of luck, but an intention to see them fulfilled in their roles.

In any field, fulfillment comes from both an individual sense of purpose, and a collective one. Your employees want to know where they fit inside your company, and how their team and their leaders will have their back. According to a PwC/CECP study, when an employee feels fulfilled, they "plan to stay at their current employer nearly three years longer in total than their less fulfilled counterparts."[13] Not only that, seven out of ten employees would consider an offer for a more fulfilling job, and one in three would do it for lower pay!

So, basically, studies make it clear that if your company is not providing your people with a sense of purpose, you've got to change something. My solution is pretty simple—create a dream that's so big, that theirs can fit inside yours.

While ensuring a sense of fulfillment in those on your team may not be 100 percent your responsibility, it must be a priority. Each of them needs to believe their contribution makes a difference. If not, your team won't care one way or another if you're moving forward.

Find employees who believe in your vision *and* are fulfilled by their role in achieving it; they'll bring you much closer to your dream.

Your Company Can Change a Community

Growing up in America as a first-generation immigrant, it was natural for me to want to support others from similar backgrounds. One of our first crew chiefs, an immigrant from Eastern Europe, was one of our hardest workers and delivered top-quality work for every job; however, he didn't speak English too well. I knew the challenges he faced in raising a family, buying a house, and wanting to build a better life for his family in a new place. As a way to show how much I valued him, I guaranteed a $160,000 a year salary, assuring him that even if there

---

[13] Building a fulfilling employee experience - CECP. Accessed November 28, 2023. https://cecp.co/wp-content/uploads/2018/12/pwc-building-a-fulfilling-employee-experience.pdf.

wasn't an opportunity for promotion, he would be recognized for how hard and how well he worked as a crew chief. Because of the language barrier, I don't think he would have been able to make that anywhere else, but he was worth it, and I knew it. I painted a picture of a dream-filled future, and it motivated him.

Our crew chief wasn't the only first-generation immigrant who was able to benefit from our company. Once we realized our potential for change in the community, we made it our mission to support other first-generation immigrants from Europe and South America.

- With a little help from my mom and her realty business, we helped immigrants get into a house within their first year in America (which if you've ever bought a house, you know how close to impossible that is). Just helping with paperwork, enabling immigrants to find the right forms, and handling some of the logistics, can truly change lives. By the end of our second year, about 50 percent of our staff were immigrants, but we didn't stop there.
- We wanted to give back to our veterans. Participating in and donating to VA (veteran's affairs) events was an awesome way for us to show our veterans we saw them for who they were, and what their sacrifice meant to us and our community.
- In 2017, when hurricane Irma destroyed over 1,500 homes, we sent a semi-truck full of donated goods to help the families impacted by the disaster. And while it cost over $2,000 to do something outside our business's purview, it wasn't the return on investment that encouraged us to send the truck, but the knowledge that we helped those who needed it.
- In 2020, when COVID shut down whole office buildings, we volunteered to disinfect firehouses for free so they could return back to work knowing their staff would be safe and healthy.

The list goes on and on... not because we've ever wanted recognition for our acts, but because we *had* to give back to our community. I've found that the more I pour into our people, the better

I feel about business. In fact, it felt so good at Romexterra that we made it a priority to put our community first. It became part of our company-wide DNA.

I'm trying to expand your idea of what a company can do for its community (plus, it's good to remind myself of what's possible!).

Dreaming in 4D

Alright, here's the exciting part. We've talked about how big the dream should be, we've discussed why it's essential to have it and how it will affect everyone around you, but now we need to set in stone exactly what yours is going to look like.

There are four elements to dreaming big—I call it the 4D Dream™:

Disneyfy It

Think about your big, huge dream for your company. Whatever dream is flashing in your head right now, go ahead and 10X it. If you think $5 million in revenue is high, shoot for $50 million. If you think you could provide jobs for 100 full time employees, dream about a *1,000-person* company. Don't get capped at what you think is possible – shoot for what is life-changing.

The more you let your doubt convince you that your company is only capable of making a certain revenue or making a small impact, the harder it will be to prove yourself wrong. This book shows you how to make that dream a reality; create a dream so big, you'll still be hungry for it in five to ten years.

Georges—this may sound crazy, but it's super important for you to do!

Date It

Let's say your dream is to sell your business for $20 million. That's amazing, and totally possible. So, when are you going to make that happen? Five years from now? Eight? Ten? Goals mean nothing if there isn't a deadline pushing you toward them.

Are you wanting to double your profits by this time next year? What shorter goals are you going to set for your team to keep you on track for that profit? Without checkpoints, there's no way to ensure you or your team will hit the goals you've set.

Predict a certain amount of growth by a specific date, then hold your team accountable to that timeline. Nothing feels better than hitting a goal by the deadline you set.

Detail It

Step into your dream, ten years from now, and then, *describe* what's going on, in detail. It may seem ridiculous at first, but I promise – the more detail you can think of, the better. Consider even seemingly pointless details like what kind of desk you'll have, what kind of cologne you'll be wearing, or what kind of haircut you'll have. Think of what pictures you'll have on your wall, how many employees you'd like to thank if you ever had to make a speech, what kind of building you'd like to work in. Dreaming isn't just about the spreadsheets or your profit – it's about the big picture, full of color and details, including smells, sounds, and sensations.

Try this: I like to use a powerful tool called "visualization," when I create my 4D Dream™. Here's how it works: Picture the scenario with a highly detailed, highly visceral imagination, as if you were in a movie. Walk through "scenes," from your future. So, walk through your future company headquarters, open the door, peak in, and smile at the receptionist. Who's working there? Where's your office? What do you see out the window? Use that same level of detail for your entire future!

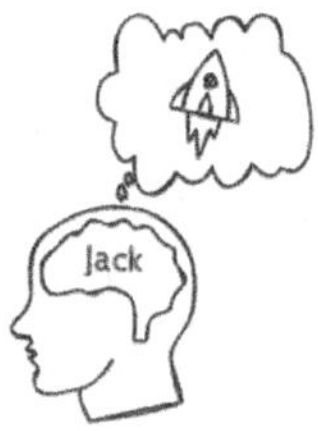

Jacks, don't slack off on this part! This helps make your dream a reality.

Draw It

After you've visualized that detailed future, map it out! Physically! Take a pen and paper, or draw it out on a tablet – whatever you can do to get what's in your head, out of it. This final step is what'll keep you on track towards your dream, as well as accountable to the excitement you felt in the beginning.

Some people like to cut out pictures and put them on a board (they call this a "vision board.") Others like to write out, in detail, their future: "I'll live in Maui, travelling two days a week, visiting my grandkids in Colorado three days a week, going to church on Sunday, going on weekly dates with my spouse..." Some people have art commissioned. My mentor Dan Martell (we mentioned him earlier!) even had his creative team write future *New York Times* articles in a mock-up of a newspaper! The point is— "draw" your future in some sort of way, that you can refer to it later.

I actually take this "draw it" step and use it for many different goals I have. For instance, I wanted to get Albi into Y Combinator—a business incubator that has helped amazing companies like Airbnb get off the ground. So, I envisioned this happening, and then, I wrote the press release prematurely! I just wanted to "draw" my future in stone. I also do this with board meetings—at the beginning of a quarter or the beginning of a year, I'll create a future board presentation for a later date, as if it already happened. "In the past quarter, we surpassed our ambitious sales goals by 10 percent." "In the past year, we received XYZ industry award." Write out the future *as if it already happened!*

As we mentioned before, we've all ridden the rollercoaster of business that can make you feel like you're on top of your game one minute, and behind the curve the next. Laying out your plans in crazy detail for future reference will make it that much easier to get psyched for the future. The more tangible your dream is, the more motivated you'll be to reach it.

The Benefit of 4D

As you continue on in this book, you'll encounter difficult choices that require trust in yourself and in what you've built. More hires, more tough decisions, more changes – but what no one ever mentioned in the end of that Spider-Man comic, is that the greater your power is and the bigger your dream gets, the easier it is to handle the responsibility that comes with them. Suddenly, big decisions become small, and huge decisions become normal, because you've planned for them.

Imagining your company in that much detail isn't just a fun exercise; it alters the way you view your own company and what you're able to achieve. Before, if you were afraid of expenses larger than X amount, my hope is that through this, you'll be able to take on decisions worth ten times that amount with confidence, knowing the big picture makes it all worth it.

Setting priorities, boundaries, and deadlines for yourself and your team enables your life and your work to thrive independently. Part of my dream was to be able to spend more time with my kids and build a stronger relationship with my family, and in defining my business goals, I was able to manage my personal goals. The more you clarify the dream for your company, the clearer the rest of your life will become.

Momentum Trigger

Create your 4D Dream™. Make sure it has the four elements of a Dreaming in 4D: Disneyfy-ed, Dated, Detailed, and physically "Drawn," or written out.

There are a lot of ways you can create a 4D Dream™—you could go cut out pictures in a magazine, you could literally paint a picture, or you could write out, in detail, what your future looks like.

But you need to really have a dream that you can watch, point to, or read over and over again.

Restorer's Recap

- Many restorers get into this business because its quick cash. They've never really thought about all that their company can be, for them, and for their community.
- Start dreaming *big.* Stop living *only* in the day-to-day and start imagining your future. Ironically, the more you live for the future, the easier today's decisions become. You'll be more motivated, feel more empowered, and you'll be more patient *if* you know you're working toward something amazing.
- "Where there is no vision, the people perish." As the ancient Jewish proverb suggests, without a big dream, you'll lose your way, and so will your employees. Employees are longing for purpose, and if you provide it, they will stay.
- Create a dreamer culture. Find the right people, then keep them through fulfilling their purpose, motivating them, and showing them how their commitment to your company will change their life.
- Have a true 4D Dream™ with the following four elements:
- Disneyfy It: However big you're thinking, think bigger.
- Date It: Give that picture a real, firm timeline.
- Detail It: What does your dream future taste and smell like?
- Draw It: Create a tangible asset that explains your future.

CHAPTER 6:
What's Your Exit Plan?

"Begin with the end in mind."
—Stephen Covey

New Tool

In this chapter, we're going to go over your exit strategy. Specifically, we're going to discuss how you want to set up your company with the same elements a buyer would want to see when considering purchasing your company from you. Those elements are:

G- growth

R- relationship

I - independence

T - thrift

Not too long ago, I spoke with a friend we'll call "Kent." Now, Kent's a fairly prolific business guy who used to also own a moving company (now, he owns a restoration company). Years before we'd met, he'd sold his moving company, piece by piece, almost entirely just for the assets involved—a few moving trucks here, dollies there, sold some of his leads, etc.

He didn't really sell his *company* to anyone, just the tangibles involved with it. Now, he knows that he was leaving a lot of money on the table. So, that's why he came to me and said, "Alex, this time, as I build my restoration company, I want to build it so I can sell it *right.*"

Kent knew that he could get much more money—I'm talking several million-dollars of *life-changing money*—if he could determine how to build and sell the company as an entire package, as a profitable asset that someone else could purchase.

In this chapter, we're going to talk about how much money your company can really be worth *if* handled correctly. I'm talking about this early in the book because I want you to have your sights set *insanely* high. I'm going to back up everything with real-life examples so you can help paint the picture of your own destiny and get a clear picture of what you want. You can think of this chapter as a follow-up to the 4D Dream.

At the end of the chapter, I'm going to also offer you a calculator that will help you find out exactly how much you need to make in your company to sell it for your desired amount.

Build Your Business to Sell

You've probably been grinding so hard in your restoration company, that you've never stopped to think, *How much could this be worth to someone else some day?*

That's actually where real-life George was at when he came to me. He was exhausted, tired of running a company, and he just wanted to get out.

"I want to sell it, Alex."

So, we dove into the numbers. Unfortunately, George's company wasn't worth much—it was only bringing in about $500,000 a year in revenue—I told him he'd essentially be selling it the same way Kent had sold his moving company, for the tangible assets involved. In other words, his business was worth his trucks and his equipment. That seemed totally unfair to George—he'd spent a decade or more working his keister off. I told him simply:

"George, look. You're not going to get what you deserve if you sell this now. But let's work together to get your business into the millions, while running smoothly, and pretty soon, you'll be able to sell it for a whole lot of money."

George and Kent aren't the only business owners who, from a place of exhaustion, try to sell a company they've spent years keeping afloat, only to find out it's worth nearly nothing.[14] That's the bad news—you may be working you rear-end off for a company that no one wants to buy. The good news? If you follow the instructions in the rest of this book, you'll own a company that's worth millions, that runs on its own, that you will only have to sell *if you want to.*

Maybe you're thinking, *I don't want to sell my business, ever, Alex!* I understand that. The good news is that it doesn't really matter! You want to set your business up *as if* you were going to sell it. Because...

A business that others want to buy is a business *you* want to run.

How do I know? Well, think of this way:

What if your business was running itself, bringing in plenty of capital every month, without much involvement from you? What if you weren't getting late-night calls or asked to deal with business (or literal!) fires all day long? What if your management team was doing the hard work, executing, and making it all happen, and you were simply acting as a strategic advisor, all while making thousands (or millions) in profit? Would *that* be a business *you* would want to buy? Of course! That's the kind of business *everyone* wants to buy. So, set up your business so it becomes one that others want to buy. Once it's running well, you can decide to sell it, or keep it. Either way, you win.

How Much GRIT Does Your Company Have?

An amazing colleague of mine, Jeff Moore, sat down and told me what acquiring buyers are looking for when they purchase companies. Jeff's company has its own fantastic history: started in 1989 by his father,

---

[14] In fact, there's an entire book written on this subject, called *Built To Sell* by John Warrillow.

ATI restoration has grown to become an *$800 million* restoration company!

Jeff is a salt-of-the-Earth guy: He loves people, he deals with you honestly, and he's a shrewd businessman. He'll *never* take advantage of you (and I doubt he's ever been taken advantage of!). By the time I caught up with him in 2023, he'd made several purchases over the previous two years to expand the ATI empire, and he'd evaluated almost *200* restoration companies by then. Based on his expertise, and my own research and experience, here's what makes a company valuable:

G-growth

R-relationship

I-independence

T-thrift

So, if this is what big players are looking for when they buy a company, this should give you insight into what to do to create a well-run business. Let's dive in.

G: Growth

Future buyers are looking to see present company growth. They want to see year-over-year increase in profits and revenue.

Jeff knows a lot of the other big players who also buy restoration companies (and yes, he says, there are quite a few). He mentioned that many of the biggest buyers won't even look at restoration companies *unless* they have year-over-year profit growth. Even if a company has great revenue, if it's making less than it was the year before, it'll have a hard time attracting a buyer.

R: Relationships

Jeff mentioned that what makes a restoration company valuable to future buyers is the *relationships* they've built, particularly the ones that bring in additional work outside of TPAs.[15]

Getting in bed with the insurance companies by becoming listed on one of their networks (TPA), is pretty easy, as Jeff noted. So, when he buys a new restoration company and adds it to the ATI family—and Jeff buys a lot of companies—he knows that he can *easily* add more TPA work. What he wants to see is a company that has deep, trusting relationships with other referral partners in the region, like plumbers and property managers.

So, if Company X gets 80 percent of its work from a TPA, and Company Y gets only 20 percent of its work from a TPA, Jeff's going to favor Company Y and pay more for it. He knows he can very easily add more TPA work.

I: Independence

If you ever want to know how valuable your company is to a prospective buyer, just ask yourself this question: *How well does my company run without me?*

If you're thinking, *My company couldn't even last a day without me!* You're not alone. Most business owners find themselves in that place

[15] Third-party administrators.

at one time or another. And don't worry—your company will be able to *sing* without you, if you follow the advice in this book.

When you want to sell your company, your independence from the operation is a huge lever—if the business can run without the owner (you) involved, it's going to be worth a lot more. An acquiring entity can't purchase your company if the entire business relies on your daily involvement. What happens if you get sick, or decide to quit as soon as the acquisition is over?

Again, wouldn't *you* rather own a company that doesn't require your hands-on involvement, too?!

This is where your people become the key that can unlock value in your company. Your business can only run without you *if* it has capable people inside of it. Here's how Jeff puts it:

> "When you buy a company, you're buying its employees."
>
> —Jeff More

And Jeff puts his money where his mouth is. Once, Jeff was looking into purchasing a company, and hopped on the phone with the owner to ask a few questions. Jeff noted that the owner didn't mention once how great his employees were. Jeff was out. He didn't even make a lowball offer. He only wants to buy the company if the employees are treated well and have a great relationship with the leadership team, so that when it gets acquired, the team mostly stays on board through the transition.

That's why Jeff's made a name for himself—over the last couple years, he's added 1,200 employees to the ATI flag through acquisitions, and guess how many left after their company was acquired by ATI?

Twelve.

Can you imagine having over a thousand employees and only a *dozen* left? That's the kind of deep-rooted team that buyers want to see in place before they buy a company, because they know the company can run independently of its owner.

T: Thrift

No, we're not talking about Goodwill shopping here. When I write *thrift,* we're talking about *capital efficiency.* Buyers aren't just looking for companies that have high revenues, but companies that have high profit margins.

Future buyers are going to look at a lot of metrics in your company, but none more so than *EBITDA.*

What the Hell Is EBITDA?

EBITDA is an accounting term used by potential company-buyers—it's a pretty fancy word, but what it *means* isn't so fancy. Technically, EBITDA stands for "earnings before interest, taxes, depreciation, and amortization." If that sounds like a lot of jargon, that's because it is. And in fact, your EBITDA is going to be (almost exactly) the same as a number you *do* know, you just don't call it that: You know that income number that your accountant gives you at the end of every year, just before they find a bunch of cool ways to (legally) lower your tax bill? I'm talking about the one that your accountant gives you as they say something like:

"Hey Alex, here's how much income you made from your restoration company this year: $____. Now, I'm going to do some financial engineering with legal depreciation and amortization that will help us claim *less* profits than that, so we can pay Uncle Sam as little on your taxes as possible."

The number that goes in that blank—that's the number I'm talking about. You're probably calling it "income" or "net income," right now. But it's essentially EBITDA—the income your accountant gives you before they wave their magic accounting wand to lower your tax bill.

Buyers call this number EBITDA, and it allows them to determine how much income your company is making every year *after* normal expenses (like payroll and such) and *before* the accountant pays the tax bill and takes some other write-offs.

I'm not going to refer to EBITDA in the rest of the book much, but just know that when you hear a company-buyer mention "EBITDA," for you, that means your income, before the accountant does all their financial engineering.

Tip: A typical net income for a restoration company hovers around 10 to 15 percent. So, that means if your company is making $3 million a year, your net income should be at least $300,000, and that would be *after* you've paid yourself a handsome salary. I suggest that restoration-company owners shoot for 15 to 20 percent net income. If you're getting anything less than 10 percent, your company is struggling. If your net income ever drops to *5* percent, you need to fix something in your business, fast.

EBITDA Multiples

OK, so here's how EBITDA factors into what a buyer will pay for your company (remember: just think "income"). They start by asking themselves the GRIT questions—what kind of growth do you have? What relationships does your company have with others in the marketplace? How independent is the company from the daily intervention for the owner? And, finally, prospective buyers will ask about your EBITDA, before offering you a multiple on that EBITDA.

If you're thinking, *What's an EBITDA multiple?*

Well, when a company is looking to purchase yours, and they want to make an offer, they'll usually offer an "EBITDA multiple," meaning they'll pay X amount times your EBITDA. So, if a company has $3 million in revenue, and their EBITDA is $300,000, a buyer might say they are willing to offer "eight times EBITDA." That would mean they were willing to pay $2.4 million.[16]

---

[16] 8 X $300,000 = $2.4 million

Before you get all tangled up in the details, remember, you need to think *EBITDA = income.* So, if a buyer is offering an "eight-X multiple," what that really means is that they are willing to pay you *eight times* the business income you get in a year. Which makes sense, because they don't care how much money is going *through* your company, they just want to know how much money they're going to make *in the end.* They basically want all your *income* for themselves, so *that's* what they're buying when they say, "EBITDA multiple."

By the way, an eight-X multiple is a pretty good, industry-wide estimate. So, to answer the question, "How much is my company worth?" the answer is (if it's running well), that your company is likely worth around eight times your EBITDA, or your income.

That's a rough industry average, and it assumes your company is running fairly well. Again, how much GRIT your company has will change your EBITDA multiple. So, let's say that you have very little GRIT, and you particularly struggle with G, growth. Well, a buyer may only be willing to offer you a three-x multiple on your EBITDA, so, that means, they may only be willing to pay you *three times* your EBITDA.

On the other hand, if you have tons of GRIT, meaning you have fantastic year-over-year growth, insanely good relationships with other trades, total independence from your business with a fantastic leadership team, and you're very capital efficient and thrifty, you may get an offer for ten or more times EBITDA. I know one guy who was offered over twelve times EBITDA because he was crushing it with his business!

Again, my goal is to help you build an excellent, strong, financially healthy restoration company that is making good profits, predictably. So, I suggest this:

If you're looking to sell your company, shoot for an eight-x multiple on your EBITDA, with an aggressive EBITDA goal of 20 percent of your profits.

First Stop: $10M in Revenue, $2M in EBITDA

Now, here's a huge caveat: Your EBITDA multiple climbs and climbs once you get to $10 million in *revenue.* Before that, honestly, your EBITDA multiple is very, very low, and many companies won't offer you anything for your company until you have $10 million in revenue.

In other words, yes, eight-times-EBITDA is a typical buyers' amount in restoration. However, your company probably isn't even worth four times EBITDA unless it's well into the millions. Prospective buyers just don't want the profits of a super small company, no matter how much GRIT it has.

My dad and I were building the plane as we were flying it, and we didn't have a plan like the Restoration Millionaire Method™, and we *still* managed to get to $10 million in revenue in under five years. Imagine how much more you can achieve with the proper tools and strategies available to you, right here in this book? Not to mention the hundreds of other resources available that have been instrumental in developing these strategies.

Even if it took you double the time, you're looking at only ten years—and by the end, with 20 percent EBITDA on a $10 million-company with an eight-x multiple, you're looking at a $16 million buyout! [17] That doesn't even include all the money you'd make along the way! How's that for a nice retirement package? You run a successful business for the next five to ten years, taking a sizeable income, then cash out with $16 million in the bank.

Nope, not a pipe dream—I did it, my father did it, and I know plenty of others who are doing it. Restoration is the untold secret gateway to becoming a millionaire. It's not overnight, and it's not a get-rich-quick scheme, but it *is* an often-overlooked business plan that can work in almost any environment, and it's nearly recession-proof, and it takes almost no capital or skills to get started.

Pretty sweet deal, huh?!

I think so.

---

[17] 20% X $10,000,000 X 8 = $16,000,000

4 Ways to Sell Your Company

So, GRIT and EBITDA, the two big things you need to know about to understand how much you could sell your company for. But did you know there are multiple *ways* to sell your company?

I have a good friend whom we'll call Steve. Now, Steve sold his Seattle-based restoration company for $10 million, but he didn't sell *all* of it. He sold the majority to private equity, and retained about 20 percent ownership, becoming president of the company. So, his 20 percent is still rapidly growing, and he cashed in and made $10 million, enough to live off of.

This is one way to sell a company: Sell the majority of it to a private equity buyer, taking a lot of your personal risk off the table and cashing in on a lot of your hard work. Meanwhile, you *still* get to keep a steady income and enough of the company that you could make more money as it grows. This is a relatively new way to sell a company, and I call it the "majority buyout." There are also at least four others:

1. **Asset sale**—This happens when you sell your restoration company for literally the assets—the phone line, the trucks, the equipment, etc. (Remember Kent, the guy we talked about at the beginning of the chapter? That's what he did with his moving company.)
2. **Majority buyout**—What Steve did: you sell the majority of your shares to someone, usually in private equity, providing you quick cash and an opportunity to maintain some control.
3. **Full buyout**—Sell the company completely and walk away with full cash value.
4. **Minority buyout** — Sell a small percentage, typically 30%, of the company and receive a cash injection to continue growing your company to even larger revenues while taking some chips off the table.
5. **Wait for buyout**—Stay in the market and sell when there's an offer that's too good to refuse.

Any of these can be a great option (except for the asset sale!) You want to sell from a position of strength, with plenty of GRIT and a high EBITDA.

After I left Romexterra, my father stayed, and you could probably put him category four "wait for buyout." Currently, he's making plenty of money (Romexterra has a pretty high EBITDA!). The company's continuing to grow (G), he has excellent relationships with his referral network (R), the company runs independently without his daily input (I), and it's running with capital efficiency, or thrift (T). So, he has a high EBITDA with lots of GRIT, meaning he's happy, and his business is running well and is financially healthy. If and when the right buyer comes along, with a high enough EBITDA multiple for his company, he'll probably take the buyout. Until then, he'll keep milking the cash cow we've created.

That's the power of running your company with GRIT, *as if* you were planning on selling it—a company that others want to buy, is a company *you* want to run.

Take on the Big Jobs

Before he left our meeting, Jeff said something really interesting. He said to never fear taking on a bigger job. He said whether it's a $10,000 mitigation job, or a $1 million commercial rebuild, to go for it. "Know who you can go to for help—your competitors, your friends, others you can subcontract to. The only thing that matters is servicing the customer."

I love Jeff's approach. This guy's running a near-billion-dollar company, and he is willing to work with anyone to serve our customers.)

I suggest following Jeff's advice—don't worry about taking on a job that's "too big." Just go for it!

Momentum Trigger

Go online to RestorationMillionaire.com/Resources and check out my calculator for building the perfect exit. This will help you determine *exactly* how much money you need to start making, this year, to cash-out with the amount you want when it's time to sell your company.

Restorer's Recap

- Most restorers don't think of their company as a sellable business that will one day be worth life-changing money. Instead, they just work until one day, something happens that forces them to change directions, so they cash-out, usually taking low-ball offers for their tangible assets.
- Instead, you can build a business that someone else would be happy to buy, because it runs independently from the ownership, and is a cash cow. That's the kind of company you want to build, then, if you want, you can sell it from a position of strength.
- Build your company with GRIT, to make it valuable to a potential buyer, and easier to run for you:
    - G: Growth
    - R: Relationships
    - I: Independence
    - T: Thrift
- "EBITDA" is an industry term that buyers use to determine how much your company is worth. It's an accounting term that means the income *before* your accountant pays taxes or does any financial engineering. You will most often hear this term brought up by company-buyers. For you, just think *income = EBITDA.*
- Your company should be making between 10 and 20 percent EBITDA (income) on your revenue. So, if your company makes $500,000 a year, your EBITDA should be between $50,000 and $100,000.
- Most buyers will pay between five- and ten-times EBITDA for your business; the higher the GRIT, the higher the EBITDA multiple will be. So, if you have low GRIT, they may give you five times EBITDA, but with very high GRIT, you may get ten times EBITDA or more.
- If you're looking to sell your company, I suggest aiming for an eight-x multiple on an EBITDA that's 20 percent of revenue.

- Most buyers won't purchase your company until you're making $10 million in revenue, and $2 million in income.

$1-5 MILLION: PROVE THE MODEL

CHAPTER 7:
Hustlers Fail at Scale

New Tool

In this chapter, we're going to talk about creating a very simple organizational chart, one that will allow you to scale into the seven- and eight- figure range. You can get to a million or more with sheer hustle, but until you learn how to delegate, you can't grow into a sustainable enterprise that will continue to grow for years to come.

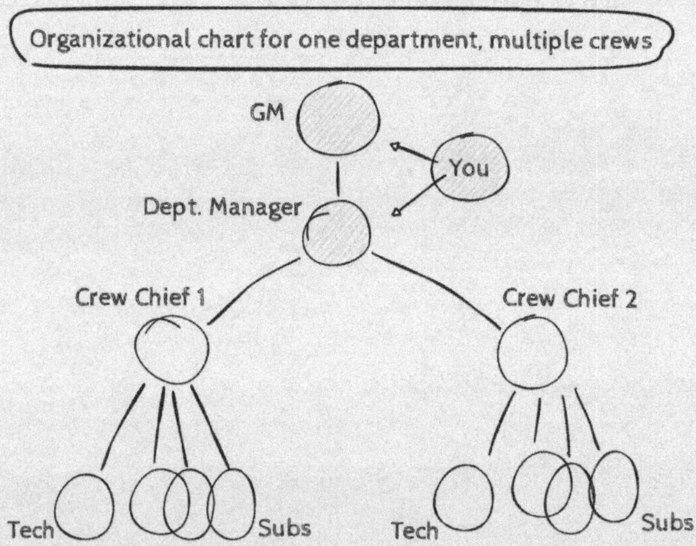

Remember when I told you that the real-life Jack called me the same week as George? George had called to sell his company (which, unfortunately, wasn't worth much at the time). George was frustrated, and so was Jack, but for very different reasons.

Jack was making *plenty* of money. But you know what? Everything was a mess. His employees were all very frustrated with him. They never knew what to do, where they were going, who was in charge, or *how* to do anything. From what it sounded like, he'd done a decent job of hiring hard workers. But from what I could tell, each project manager had their own unique system of billing and collecting. Each technician did their job their way. You'd think with all that freedom, employees were happy. They weren't. The company was suffering from chaos, and Jack was nearly about to suffer a heart attack! He was stressed, overworked, and outgunned. He was running from job to job, fixing little problems. He was also scurrying between houses selling *new* work.

The guy was making $7 million a year in revenue. By then, there's no way he should have been involved with every sale, but he still was. By then, Jack definitely should have had some standardized way of completing tasks and billing invoices, but he didn't. By then, he should have had an office manager who was answering the phone, organizing files, and doing all the administrative stuff that Jack *never* did, the sorts of "small" things that can eat up a lot of time if you do them, and eat up more time if you don't.

Simply put? Poor Jack called me because he was *drowning*. He'd hit a moment of crisis, and, just like George, he wanted out.

Jack was having a hard time, because he'd gotten to where he was with hustle, so he kept hustling. And hustle is brilliant, but only to a point. And Jack had hit it.

Hustlers Fail at Scale

You can do a lot with hustle. You can start a company, you can put up the framing in a house, clean out the water in the basement, or build a company up to seven figures. But you know what you *can't* do with hustle alone? Build a company into eight or more figures.

Jack had hit his hustle ceiling. It didn't matter how much more he hustled, his company wasn't going to grow anymore. In some ways, he was back on the Reactive Rollercoaster™. He had grown a sizeable company (even though he was working far too much). He had great revenue and a fairly great team (even though they were upset).

But the problem was that what had helped him become the owner of a $7 million company, would never help him own a $10 million+ company. What's worse, he was ready to throw in the towel—so stressed from having to put his hand in every pot, with no leadership helping put out fires in the business, Jack was all but *done.*

"What Got You Here, Won't Get You There"

World-famous executive leadership coach Marshall Goldsmith wrote a book called *What Got You Here Won't Get You There.* Even in the title, there's a lot we can glean.

If you've used a hammer to drive nails into wood, it's pretty amazing how you can get better and better with that hammer. With practice, you can become faster and more efficient at building with that one simple tool. But remember the first time you saw a nail *gun?* Those bad boys are on a whole other level.

Hustle is like a hammer. It works, for a while. But there's a level of scalability and leadership you can attain that's an order of magnitude greater than anything you can achieve with hustle alone.

It's really hard to let go of the mindset that "more hustle = more success." Because, for a long time, *it did.* If you've started a business, grit was your friend as you trudged through the early days of difficulty. If you've grown a business, hustle was by your side as you stayed up late and took on jobs that were out of your league. Hustle is a great companion, for a long time. But somewhere along the way, you have to say goodbye to him. Because...

Hustlers fail at scale.

You simply can't build a $100 million-dollar company without a leadership team. There's no way that you can scale past a certain point without delegating and depending on others. You can only do so much work for so long, until you run out of time in the day or energy in your life. That's why...

Hustlers fail at scale.

You can't be in two places at once. You don't have more than twenty-four hours in a day. You simply can't juggle more and more tasks without having help. You can work hard and fast. But at some point...

Hustlers fail at scale.

From Player to Coach

The first part of this book focused on getting you to your first $1 million. First off, getting any company started is a big deal, much less into the millions. If you've made it there, sincerely, congrats. That's huge! But now, it's time to learn how to prove your business model—you've got to take what's been working and refine it enough so you can copy-paste, copy-paste, over and over again.

Oh, and here's a clue—you can't copy and paste *you.* What you *can* copy-paste, is your training, your procedures, and your way of doing business. Well, you can copy-paste all that *if* you have the right systems, procedures, and team in place. We'll get to *all* that in this second part of the book, but in this chapter, we're going to start with your team. We're going to talk about how to let go of perfection and learn to love 80 percent, and then we're also going to show you how restorers can set up an easily replicable organizational chart, one that you can copy-paste, over and over again.

I know, "organizational chart" doesn't exactly roll of the tongue. In fact, it sounds like something that would drive most Jacks into utter boredom! Don't worry—we'll make this conversation fun.

Get to 80

So, before we talk about your organizational chart, I want to pound on this "hustlers fail at scale situation."

Jack and George, and probably *all* business owners, struggle with one big issue: They think it's *impossible* to find someone who's as good as them at anything. I get that. To get to where you are, you've relied on your wits and innate skills to get you by. But somewhere along the way, you probably built up this mentality that no one can do what you do. You might have told yourself in the past (or this morning) that there doesn't seem to be anyone else who can ___ like you…

- Sell like you
- Market like you
- Appease the customer like you
- Care about the business as much as you
- Manage multiple projects as efficiently as you

But you know what? It doesn't really *matter* if they do it just as well as you do. In fact, you're not even aiming for that.

Whenever I hear those voices inside my head, the ones that tell me my employees can't do X as well as I can, I defer to Dan's[18] words of wisdom:

"80 percent done by someone else is 100 percent freaking awesome." [19]

Dan explains how perfection is an impossible goal. When delegating tasks to others, don't even aim for 100 percent. Instead, aim for 80. This target gives your team the chance to breathe easy if they happen to make a mistake, and it allows you to sit back and relax.

---

[18] Yes, Dan Martell again!

[19] Martell, Dan. 2023. *Buy Back Your Time: Get Unstuck, Reclaim Your Freedom, and Build Your Empire.* Penguin.

The benchmark of 80 percent is a great target to have—if an employee can't get to at least 80 percent, then they may not be a great fit. If they're getting 80 or above, you should be *stoked!*

Think about it this way. Let's say that you're tired of having to do all the bill collection. Even with your 48-Hour Rule™, if you're making tons in revenue, bill collection can be difficult. So, you should make all your crew chiefs or project managers handle the invoicing and collection. But you might think, *Yeah, but Susan won't remember to text, email,* ***and*** *call. Plus, Larry always misses some items on his invoices...*

Look, that may all be true. But let it go—don't shoot for *perfection* from Susan or Larry. Instead, ask yourself this: *How much easier would my life be if I only had to do the last 20 percent of this task?*

Maybe no one is quite as good at you are at sales, but I bet they can do 80 percent as good as you can—so, you can have someone handle all the sales besides the largest jobs.

Perhaps no employee you can find is as good as you are at answering the phone. OK, but I bet someone can answer it every time *almost* as well as you can, so, overall, wouldn't that be a net win, since you've got other things to do?

Maybe Susan or Larry misses some small things on your invoices, but, if suddenly, you only had to get involved one out of every five times, wouldn't that be *amazing?*

Don't shoot for perfection.

Shoot for 80 percent.

Organizational Charts Are Sexy

In the beginning days of Romexterra, we felt pretty good about ourselves – proud of how we were growing the company, comfortably paying our employees, and finally making good profit. But in order to grow past a couple million in revenue, we had to start building up from our foundation. It was time to prove (and improve) the model. We hired a consultant who introduced my dad and me to our need for an organizational chart. Not only did we need one, but we also needed to know how to *create* one.

Why do you need to create organizational chart? Well, without an organizational chart, you simply can't keep scaling up.

If you're a Jack, who's focused almost entirely on hustling, your "organizational chart" probably doesn't look like any sort of chart at all—your company is probably just a collection of people running around, working as hard and as fast as they can, until they quit or get fired. Honestly, I have some respect for that! You've got to start *somewhere,* right?

Well, I'm going to give you a very simple organizational chart that will allow you to scale upward. It really only has four levels. Here it is:

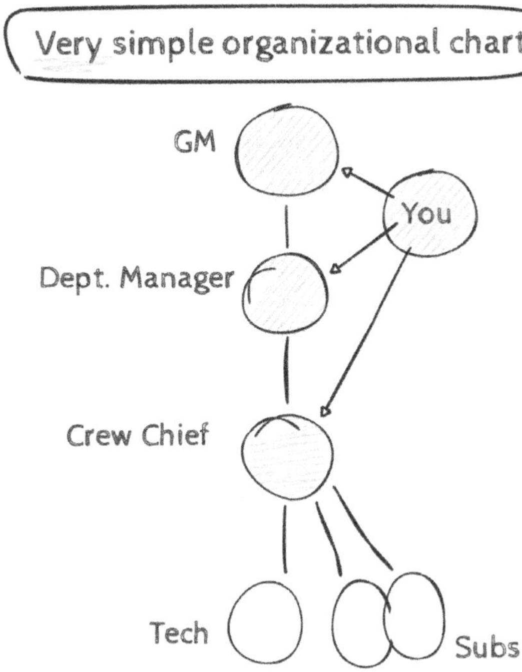

Essentially, with this organizational chart, you can create an infinite number of crews, and scaling up becomes clear—- there's only three levels between one end of the organizational chart and you. So, you start out as the crew chief, the department manager, and the general manager, with any technicians and/or subs "under" you. That's the model, and it's very simple.

Eventually, if you follow the Fishing Holes model, you'll have plenty of work coming in, and you'll need a new crew. So, you duplicate your small crew—you get another crew chief, who will likely need their own truck, their own technician, and maybe their own subcontractors that they're responsible for. You may remain the crew chief over your crew, or you could become the department manager and give over your crew to someone else, as well. So, now, your chart, will probably look something like this:

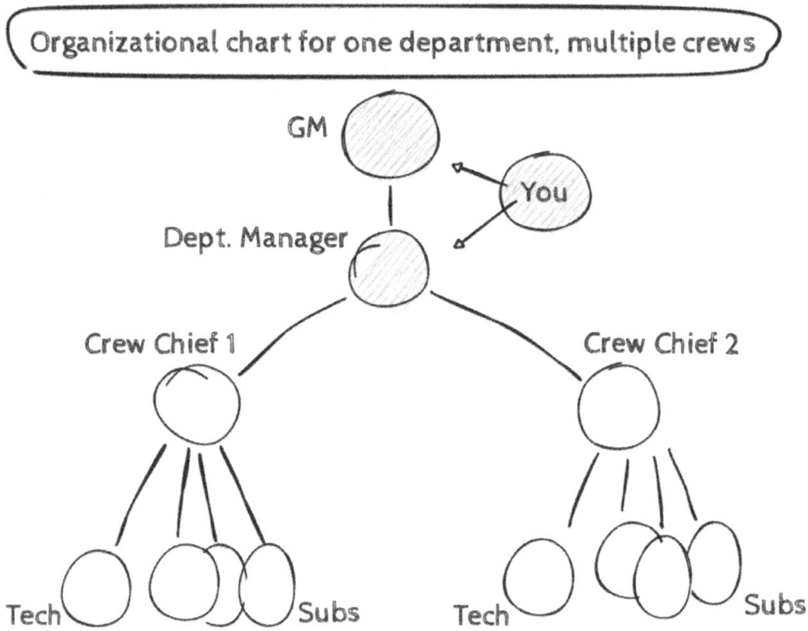

Now, you can keep replicating more and more and more crews, each crew following the same basic model of crew chief + technician (and/or subcontractors).

Now, this works well with only one line of business—let's say emergency services, and, per the Restoration Millionaire Method™, you should stay with one service until you get to Fishing Hole IV (which happens around $5 million).

But, I know that you like to look ahead (and plus, there's a chance you already have other services). So, in that case, let me show you how the organizational chart works with more offerings. As your company gets bigger and bigger, you'll want to organize your crews into official departments by service offering, even if you remain as the only "department manager" over each area. So, take a look at this chart, which assumes there are three different departments (say roofing, emergency services, and fire rebuilds):

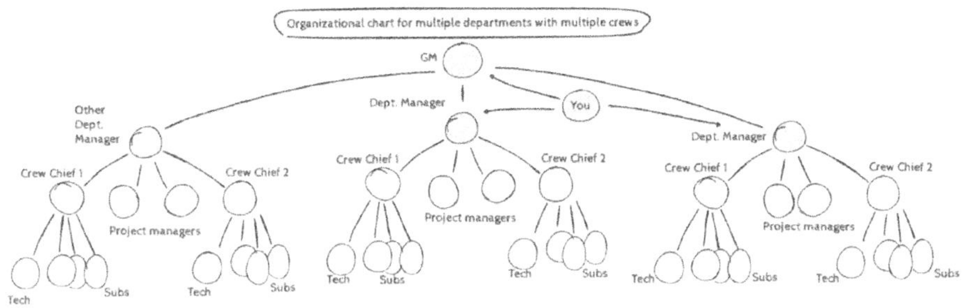

Notice, you may still technically be the "department manager" of each area of your company, or you may have only some of the department manager positions filled by other people. Also, notice that, at some point, and almost certainly when you have multiple departments, you'll have *project managers,* positions that typically emerge after you've got at least two crew members inside of a department. So, let's say that you have two departments, Fire & Smoke and Water Damage. Once either of these grows so large that you have two crews or more in either department, you'll probably want a project manager to be there.

Technically, project managers are not really "over" the crew chiefs, so the word *manager* is a bit out of place. However, they are usually the people who sell the job, and handle the invoicing and collecting so that the crew chiefs can keep working on the next job.

Project managers become vitally important as you get bigger, and they help keep the jobs streamlined, and paid on time. While I only have them in the third chart above, you may need them earlier.

Once you've gotten so large that you *also* need back-of-house stuff, your organizational chart will probably look slightly more complex, with a back-of-house staff, and that will look something like this:

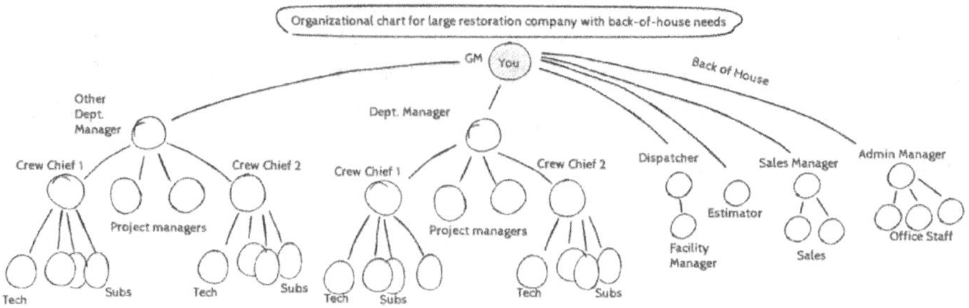

Three Guidelines for Organizational Charts

In general, you—the business owner—are going to move "up" the organizational chart and hire someone to fill your position. So, you'll start out as crew chief, department manager, and general manager. Then, you'll move up to department manager and general manager and hire someone to handle crew chief. Then you'll move up to only the general manager and hire department managers.

That's the general path. Honestly though, it doesn't always work so seamlessly.

You'll notice I didn't attach the organizational charts to highly specific revenue goals. There's a reason for that—your first instinct might be to fill positions at a specific monetary point in your business, or to fill the cheapest position first. But honestly, that's not the point.

You may even need to hire a back-of-house person early on, even before you have more than one department. That's because the idea isn't to follow a specific organizational chart on a specific deadline.

I present these organizational charts as a sort of general advice, not as a hard-and-fast plan you have to follow. I like to think of Captain Barbosa in *Pirates of the Caribbean* who said that the pirate's code of rules is a collection of more "guidelines than actual rules."

Georges, don't get so caught up in following "the rules" that you miss the point of the rule. Make your organizational chart work for you and your business!

So, here are the three *guidelines* for your organizational charting:

1) The owner should move *up* the ladder as soon as possible.

2) No one should have more than eight direct reports, ever.

3) Hire someone into a role as soon as your company is experiencing the problems that role should solve.

Let me explain each of these in a little more detail:

1: The Owner Should Keep Moving Up

Your goal is to move up the organizational chart as much as possible.

Currently, you may be wearing every hat in the business. Even if you're not wearing *all* of them, I bet you're wearing too many: You may sell the job, dry the carpets, send the bill, talk to insurance, and cash the checks. Wherever you're at, move up as soon as you're able to so that you have more time for the strategic decisions that affect your entire company.

When I talked with Jack, he was still selling jobs. At $7 million in revenue, that should have been someone else's job, and until Jack got out of it, he wouldn't be able to think about bigger-ticket items, like marketing, referral partnerships, etc.

And, remember GRIT? The I stands for *independence.* You won't be able to sell your business, and it won't be worth anything to investors, until you have some freedom from it. Plus, do you really want to be the only person in your business with all of the answers? I mean, if you can't go on vacation for a week without getting a dozen phone calls about big issues, you're not living in freedom at all. Here's how I like to say it:

If the owner's vacation causes a problem, then there's a problem!

We'll talk more about what it means to think strategically in chapter twelve, but now, know this: keep moving up the organizational chart, removing hats as you climb.

2: No One Manages More Than 8 Direct Reports

When my father and I first started Romexterra, we quickly ended up with fifteen to twenty employees—and we were the only managers. It was getting crazier and crazier—each new employee added tons of stress, not because they were poor employees, but because it was just too many people to manage.

Plenty of leadership books and management programs will tell you that most people should have about six to eight "direct reports." A "direct report" is someone for whom you're immediately and officially responsible for. At Romexterra, we only had two layers in our company:

Layer one: Managers (my dad and I).

Layer two: Everyone else.

With layers like that, every time we hired someone new, my dad and I became immediately responsible for a new direct report. That's why our business consultant helped us put in a very simple organizational chart with a couple more managerial layers, just like the one we showed you earlier. Voila! By adding in another layer or two, everyone in the company suddenly only had six to eight people for whom they were directly responsible.

When you arrange your organizational chart, however you do it, ensure one thing happens: no one is *directly responsible* for more than eight people at any given time.

3: Hire Someone As Soon You Have the Problems They Can Solve

Your first instinct might be to fill the cheapest position, for the fear of expanding your budget, or because you simply want to knock out the easiest positions to fill, first. But instead, hire for the problems needing to be fixed, even if that creates difficult financial decisions.

You've probably heard "have three months' worth of expenses in the banks at all times." That's a nice thought, but honestly, I don't think that's always the best rule.

While you want to be as prudent as possible, honestly, you're not always going to have a nice three months of cash padding in the bank, especially in restoration where the money comes in lump sums. But as long as you're following the 48-Hour Rule™, and consistently collecting money, it's OK to hire someone when you know the money's coming in. So, don't hire someone just because you do or do not have all the money or because you are or are not at a certain revenue level in your organization. Instead, simply ask yourself, *What are the problems we're having?*

- If you're having a problem in sales, hire someone to solve your sales problem.
- If you're having a problem with your technicians, maybe you need a crew chief.
- If you're having a problem with collections, maybe you should hire someone just to handle collections.

Spending more money always feels risky, but more often than not, it's the next step you have to take to alleviate your biggest source of pain. Don't settle for the cheapest hires -- get creative, think outside the box to pay for the folks you need. If you don't have all the cash, consider opening a line of credit until your new revenue is able to cover the cost (or, go check out my CREDIT system in chapter thirteen).

After my dad and I brought on the business consultant, they helped us first create a simple organizational chart. Next, it became obvious what we needed to do; we needed to hire someone in collections, because collecting money was our biggest pain point.

If my dad and I had just been focused on the numbers, we would have gotten discouraged—it felt like hiring a collections role was going to cause us to take a big financial hit. But, it was what we needed to do to grow. So, thankfully, we listened to the consultant, and hired for the collections position. Once my dad and I filled that seat, it became that much easier to fill in the next, as my dad and I got more comfortable letting go of direct responsibility. Our names, which once filled every spot on the organizational chart, were gradually getting replaced. Eventually, the only ones we occupied were at the top. Your business should follow a similar pattern of growth.

Every new hire (and investment in new technology for that matter) is a bet on your eventual success, and bets often take about six to nine months for the cost to even out. Whether it's a new production manager or the purchase of a new truck, get comfortable with expanding your budget to enable your company's growth.

Move Up

When Romexterra reached $2 million in revenue, we began looking forward to our future. What would $10 million be like? $20 million? It only became possible with the right staff and the best structure. But having the right structure only gets you on the right path. Not only does it take **patience as an entrepreneur**, but **endurance as a coach,** and **discipline as a manager**.

Patience, though it may be an obvious virtue in your personal life, is also a must for any entrepreneur looking to grow. Why? Because every investment, every hire, has a long rate of return. As I mentioned, a new hire or piece of equipment doesn't always become lucrative until several months in.

And with patience, grows endurance. Only you and your top management team can see the light at the end of the tunnel. When that light becomes a bit harder for them to see, it's your job, as their coach, to keep your head up and encourage your team to do the same. Your risk may be the highest, but your drive is also the greatest.

And finally, when you've had patience, and when you've endured, you will have gained a discipline unlike any other. Trust in the organizational chart you've built; it's what will boost you to the next phase of replicating your business.

Now that we've established the need for organizational charts, the next chapter will show you how to make sure every job gets done the right way, every time.

Momentum Trigger

For this chapter, there are two steps to your Momentum Trigger. If you're pleased with your current organizational chart, skip to step two:

1: If Your Organizational Chart Needs Some Love...

If your organizational chart is non-existent or unhelpful, let's get it set up right. Using our simple four-layer organizational chart as the starting point, go through your entire company and organize it so that the following guidelines are apparent:

- Make room for the owner to move up ASAP.
- Ensure no one has more than eight direct reports.

If you want a simple worksheet to help you set up your organizational chart, you can go to: RestorationMillioniare.com/Resources. Once you've organized your company, go on to step two:

2: Once Your Organizational Chart Is Set Up Well...

Think of the one place where your company is experiencing the most pain. Usually, this is the area that is causing cashflow problems or time leaks—either cash isn't flowing correctly because of this problem, or you're spending hours every week trying to solve it. Now, once you know the problem, *hire to fix it.*

Put some time on the calendar, right now, to hire someone who can solve that problem for you so you're no longer being held back by it. And remember, an experienced professional *will* cost you money.

Restorer's Recap

- **Hustler's fail at scale.** You can grow a great company up to a certain point with nothing but hustle. But you know? You can't scale it into eight figures with hustle. For that, you'll need to learn how to depend on others.
- Many business owners have a hard time "letting go" of responsibilities, because they think, *No one does ____ as well as I do!* That may be true. But remember what Dan Martell says:

80% done by someone else is 100% freaking awesome.

- Organizational charts unlock the key to growth. Instead of thinking "hustle," think, *Who do I need?*
- First, build a *simple* organizational chart that will allow you to infinitely scale the same basic chart in every department in every area of your restoration business. First, you'll be wearing all the hats. But then, you'll be able to move up, out of those roles.
- Organizational charts are guidelines. Instead of using the following organizational charts as hard and fast rules, follow these three principles when making your charts:

1) The Owner Should Keep Moving Up
2) No One Manages More Than 8 Direct Reports
3) Hire Someone As Soon You Have the Problems They Can Solve

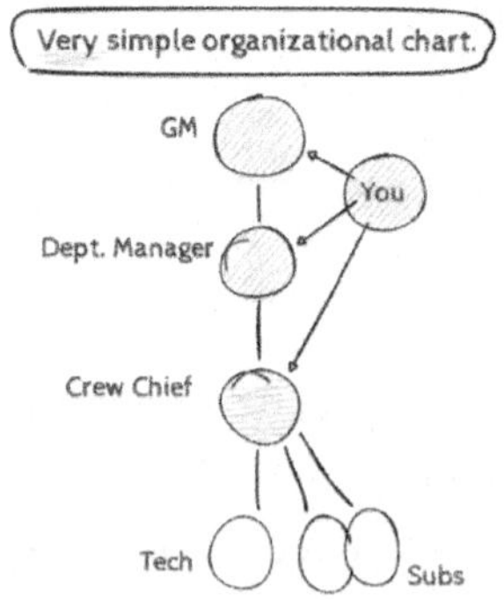
Very simple organizational chart.
GM
You
Dept. Manager
Crew Chief
Tech
Subs

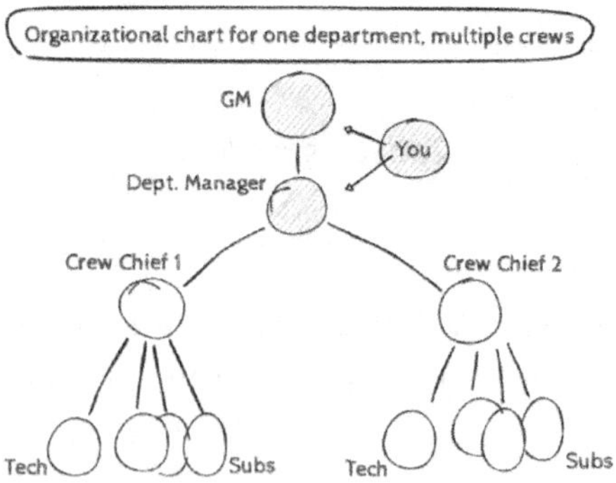
Organizational chart for one department, multiple crews
GM
You
Dept. Manager
Crew Chief 1
Crew Chief 2
Tech
Subs
Tech
Subs

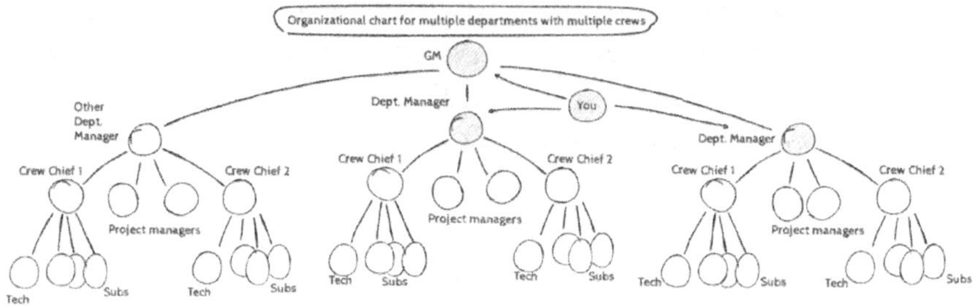
Organizational chart for multiple departments with multiple crews
GM
You
Other Dept. Manager
Dept. Manager
Dept. Manager
Crew Chief 1
Crew Chief 2
Project managers
Tech
Subs

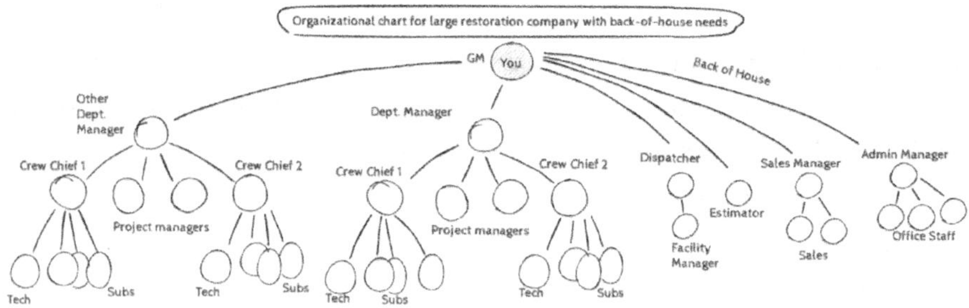
Organizational chart for large restoration company with back-of-house needs
GM
You
Back of House
Other Dept. Manager
Dept. Manager
Crew Chief 1
Crew Chief 2
Project managers
Tech
Subs
Dispatcher
Estimator
Facility Manager
Sales Manager
Sales
Admin Manager
Office Staff

CHAPTER 8:
3 SOPs to Help You Breathe Easy

"If you can't describe what you are doing as a process, you don't know what you're doing."
-W. Edwards Deming

New Tool

In this chapter, we're going to discuss SOPs, or standard operating procedures. SOPs help explain *how things are done,* from a to z. You could use an SOP for something simple, like "how to use our system to send an invoice," or, you could create an SOP for an entire department, one that may have a bunch of smaller SOPs inside of it.

You can find a full SOP in the back of the book for all of water mitigation, or you can go online to: RestorationMillionaire.com/resources and find a few examples there.

Here's an example of a *portion* of an SOP, which focuses on how to handle a water mitigation call:

Lead Qualification

The Call Taker receives all phone calls and determines qualified leads. The qualifications must include all of the following:

1) The customer needs an emergency service provided by the company (YOUR SERVICES). This includes any repairs when appropriate.
2) The customer is within an **X-mile** radius of **Your Address.**
3) The customer identifies themselves as the homeowner or authorized by the homeowner.
4) The customer is willing to allow **Your Company** to perform a property inspection of the damages before giving a price.

The Call Taker promises the customer that a project manager will arrive on the scene within the "lead time" on the dispatch board. This "lead time" is set by the Dispatcher. From that moment forward, the project manager will assist from there.

A Lesson From Poker

A few years ago, I played poker against the house at a casino—it was one of those games where the rules are very constrained, and you play only against the dealer. The game was some version of Texas Hold 'em.

I know the basics of the game and the hands, but I wasn't exactly a professional, so I bet and played with relatively little strategy, until a lady sat down next to me. She sat with her cheat sheet (which I was surprised the casino allowed her to have!). Her cheat sheet told her exactly how to bet with what pocket cards. There was a rule for having only one ace, for having a king, for having queen-six, and so on.

I started following her playbook, and interestingly, everything suddenly became very, very predictable. By following a system, I had a very consistent way of playing—I lost some hands and won many of them. I knew when to fold, when to hold. Instead of going off "my gut" or "my instincts," I simply followed the time-tested data. While the system couldn't predict what would happen every hand, if I followed her cheat sheet, I knew about how my cards would pan out over time. I wasn't just asking myself, *How do I feel about six-seven off-suit?* Instead, I was following a predictable strategy.

And that's the power of having a playbook—you can get rid of all the emotion, and follow a peaceful, predictable path toward winning. And that's what we're going to discuss in this chapter.

The Cheat Sheets for Business

If you've ever seen the movie *21*, based on the true story found in the book, *Bringing Down the House,* you'll notice something similar—calculated card players who win over time have a systematic way of playing certain card games.

Smart businesses have something similar, playbooks, if you will, on how to win. Systematized processes that allow them to pump out predictable outcomes over and over and over again.

Think about when you go into your favorite chain coffee shop or fast-food joint. I love Chipotle. You can go into Chipotle anywhere they have a location in the United States and get the same burrito with the same ingredients.

That's because Chipotle has their own "playbooks," or, as they're more officially called in business, standard operating procedures (SOPs).

They have an SOP on how to make burritos, an SOP on how to train staff, and (probably) even an SOP to put up a new store—Starbucks famously would put almost all stores on *corner* lots, because, according to their SOP, corner spots in buildings allow them to have a drive through and standout more.

Most small businesses have very few, if any SOPs, and honestly, not having them is typically one of the main reasons they're so small—if they could just learn to systematize their offerings, so that customers know what to expect, and employees know what to do, then the small businesses would often get larger from that alone.

But instead, hustlers often start small businesses, and remember, *hustlers fail at scale.*

By nature, entrepreneurs are good problem-solvers. So, they approach every situation with an open mind, looking for a creative solution. I totally get that. I'm the same way! And in fact, *most* entrepreneurs in every business are just like that. But you know who's not like that? Most employees, even really, really hard-working ones. Most people don't enjoy not having a how-to manual, and they don't like having to figure out new things on a moment-by-moment basis, which is why they want to work for you, and not for themselves. You should use that to your advantage and make sure you're not stressing your employees out—just offer them some step-by-step instructions for some of the biggest tasks, that way, they can save their creativity for the tasks that do need them.

You can't systemize everything in every business all the time. There will always be situations that require out-of-the-box thinking, but much of what you do, is repeatable, particularly in restoration.

Most carpets are dried the same way, most documentation needs to be filled out the same way, and most insurance companies need the same forms. Everything, from how to fill out a form, to how to sell a job to a customer, to where to put away the tools, can have an SOP. And honestly, the more systemized your business is, the more time you'll save, the more headaches you'll avoid, and the more predictable everything will become.

Think about it this way...

What if you could predict with 90 percent certainty how much your sales would be next month?

What if all your employees filled out the same forms every time when they finished a job?

What if every employee learned the same exact material within the first month of working for you?

Would your business be better off? I'll bet it would be!

An unfortunate reality in the restoration world is many business owners assume SOPs are a waste of time. Either they complain that the information constantly needs to be updated so they don't even attempt it, or they believe experience is the best (and only) teacher. I've heard a dozen excuses from restoration colleagues for why SOPs are more work than they're worth but trust me–by the end of this chapter, you'll have clear guidelines for *how* to build an SOP, and *why* you need to implement them as soon as possible.

***

An SOP is a step-by-step gameplan that tells your employees exactly what to do, what to click, what to say. And with one, they feel empowered to do their part on your team.

For you, you'll see three things in your business as soon as you start using SOPs:

1: Consistency

SOPs remove unnecessary emotion from the equation. Instead of reacting to each situation independently, SOPs will tell you how to respond (literally the exact words to say), creating more consistent decisions from your employees to your clients. In Texas Hold 'em, if you have a 4-5 of hearts, you wouldn't stay in the game just because you see a 6 of hearts on the river. Rather, you follow the guidelines, fold your cards, then save your bets for the next round.

If you come across a situation not already addressed in your SOP, update it to ensure each similar situation is handled the same for future occurrences.

2: Accountability

SOPs make your expectations black and white. Coworkers at any time can reference live SOPs when conflict needs to be resolved. Similarly, if you rely on procedure more than skill, all technicians will be able to compete at the same level, which will make your business more effective overall.

3: Predictability

SOPs will add a whole bunch of predictability to your business. If you want to get off the Reactive Rollercoaster™, there may be no faster way than using SOPs.

I find this to be especially true in *sales.* Sales can be a... well, a big pain for us restorers. Often times, our sales look lumpy because we're waiting on a big check, hustling a big job, or coming in right after a big fire. It can *feel* like we have no control over sales, but I can tell you from experience, and from working with hundreds of other restoration founders all over the country, that this simply isn't true.

In fact, this industry is so predictable, that's why I have a calculator that can predict how many homes will make insurance claims for fires, wind & hail, and water damage!

So, that means your sales *can absolutely be predictable.*

At Romexterra, we ended up with a sales program that became highly predictable because of our sales SOP. We could predict, with relative accuracy, how much money we would make each quarter and each month.

If a big job happened to come through, well, that was just icing on the cake.

Think of how much more relaxed you'd be if you knew exactly how much more work you'd need to do, or how many more people you'd need to hire, to hit X goal?

You Can't Get to the Next Level Without SOPs

I know putting in SOPs sounds... *boring,* unexciting, and time-consuming. But you know what? You'll never get to the next level without them. I can't predict *exactly* where the breakdown will be, but I can say for a fact that I know a ton of $30 million+ restoration companies, and *all* of them have SOPs. And I can tell you that all the companies that *don't* have them are under $10 million!

Not only that, but you know who else is being affected by you not having SOPs? Your family. You're getting phone calls when you should be having dinner, and answering emails when you should be playing with your kids or hanging out with your girlfriend, simply because your employees don't have a source of truth they can refer to on what to do when.

So, let's get to that next level with the SOPs.

Jacks! I know SOPs sound silly to you. But let me put it to you this way: What if you could double your hustling efforts? Sound bad-ass? Get some dang SOPs!

The Few SOPs You Need

SOPs will mitigate the majority of any entrepreneur's issues. Now, you could go *crazy* here with SOPs—I bet all my Georges are just so excited right now. But truthfully, there are three main SOPs you need. Sure, you can add more as you go along, but if you put in these three *now*, you'll increase your revenue by 10-20 percent within a quarter. And decrease your stress by 30 percent... *at a minimum.*

Here's the three categories of SOPs you should start with:

- **Job-Flow SOP:** how one project looks at various phases
- **Sales & Marketing SOP:** how your salespeople can generate business and make sales
- **Employee Onboarding SOP:** standards for hiring & training; preparing candidates to go out and represent your brand.

Again, these SOPs made our business consistent, accountable, and predictable. At Romexterra we could've had all the luck in the world, but without proper systems to maintain the momentum of our business, we would never have grown beyond a couple million in revenue.

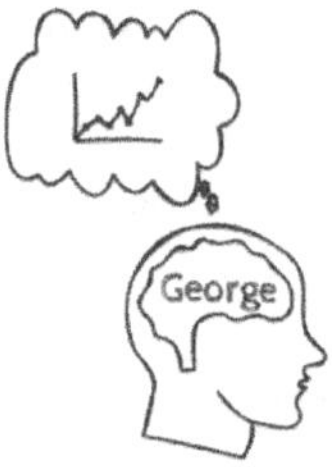

Georges: Don't get carried away here! I know—you've probably read every book about EOS[20] and you're just itching to build SOPs for *everything.* But the truth is, you probably only need a few SOPs to get going! Don't make SOPs for everything; make them for the handful of tasks that you need to do repeatedly.

1: Job-Flow SOP

Most restoration companies have one to five main tasks that they perform repeatedly—let's say you have three: water mitigation, tear-outs, and fire rebuilds.

Consider what the one to five main tasks you have are, and build out an entire SOP for the whole flow of work in that department. I'm talking, start *all the way at the beginning...*

How does the call come in?

Who goes where?

Who makes the sale?

What lead is considered qualified?

What do you do if a lead isn't qualified?

Who gets the homeowner to sign the project?

When does the project start?

What are the main categories of types of jobs?

What happens differently if it's category A, versus Category B? [21]

---

[20] EOS stands for Entrepreneurial Operating Systems, and it embodies a method of running your business with set procedures.

[21] I have an entire water mitigation SOP built out already. Check out in the back of the book, or online at RestorationMillionaire.com/resources

We'll talk more about *how* to create, draw, and map out your SOPs here shortly, but this should get you thinking.

2: Sales & Marketing SOP

Sales & marketing needs an SOP to determine...

How do you bring in new sales through the door?
How many times do you visit with referral parties every day?
If you have a referral program... how does this work?
Who calls whom, when?

Most restorers don't believe me when I tell them that they can actually *predict* what their sales are going to be with a well-executed sales & marketing SOP!

3: Employee Onboarding SOP

For a while, I had all my new technical, specialists, and crew chiefs shadow seasoned veterans at Romexterra. *Who is better to teach a newbie, than a pro?* I thought.

But then, several months later, the new employees *were still* having tons of problems and making goofy mistakes. I had some really great people on board, so I knew it must have been the training, and it was. Even with the fantastic veterans teaching our newer employees, we still needed SOPs.

We put in a checklist of what every new employee needed to learn to get signed off on in their area, along with SOPs that reinforced what they were learning on the job from the veterans, and voila! Our training program was taken to the next level.

SOPs are a great supplement to real-world training, and plus, it helps with accountability—once it's written down, no employee can say they didn't know. They can only say they didn't read it.

And that's it—those are the three categories of SOPs you need. I say "categories," because you may have two or more job-flow SOPs, and then you may have different sales SOPs, depending on the department.

And, the same is true with your new employee onboarding SOPs if you have different lines of business.

If you want to see my water mitigation SOP, check it out in the back of the book (or online); it's pretty long, so it doesn't make sense to put the whole thing right here, but here's a quick screen shot of one section, lead qualification, to give you an idea of the final product:

Lead Qualification

The Call Taker receives all phone calls and determines qualified leads. The qualifications must include all of the following:

5) The customer needs an emergency service provided by the company (YOUR SERVICES). This includes any repairs when appropriate.
6) The customer is within an **X-mile** radius of **Your Address.**
7) The customer identifies themselves as the homeowner or authorized by the homeowner.
8) The customer is willing to allow **Your Company** to perform a property inspection of the damages before giving a price.

The Call Taker promises the customer that a project manager will arrive on the scene within the "lead time" on the dispatch board. This "lead time" is set by the Dispatcher. From that moment forward, the project manager will assist from there.

Now, how did I get to this point? I started by drawing, actually. And you can, too. Here's how to make your own, first, SOP:

How to Create Your First SOP

SOPs do not have to be overly complex documents. Rather, they are like recipes—simple instructions anyone should be able to follow. Take Gordon Ramsey's *Quick and Delicious: 100 recipes to cook in 30 minutes or less.* In it, he offers step-by-step instructions that require no more skill than someone who's never fried an egg. You don't have to understand the history of the dish to make it properly. Simply, follow the steps in order, pay attention to the measurements, and look at the pictures for guidance. Ramsey's cookbook is successful because he makes his readers feel as if they can cook *just like him.*

This is what you should strive for when writing your SOPs: clear step-by-step directions that give your new employees confidence that they can be as successful as you.

And you start that by *drawing.*

A: Sketch the SOP on Paper

I usually take out a piece of paper (or use my iPad) and just start writing out "do this, then this, etc." Sometimes, I use boxes for each step of the process, then fill them in, and draw arrows to connect each step.

I like to think of it like a movie script—I imagine myself picking up the call, making the sale, drying the carpet... doing whatever I'm trying to explain, and then I walk my character through the whole experience, from beginning to end.

B: Put the SOP in a Shareable Drive

Once I have an idea of how I want my SOPs to look, I start taking my shapes and boxes, and putting them in linear format in some sort of electronic, shareable file, where I can keep my documents easily accessible to anyone. This has to do with both accessibility and updatability:

When you use a "live" document that gets revised for accuracy frequently, it stays up-to-date and usable. As a bonus, of course, you can also attach links within your live documents, video clips, etc.

C: Be Detailed

Your SOPs can never be too granular. The more specific you get, the more consistent outcome your employees will have.

For instance, in one of our SOPs, we have a step for sales that says, "after you knock on a homeowner's door the first time, take three steps back."

We know, from experience, that after homeowners have experienced a huge loss, they're typically on edge, and having a stranger show up at their door makes them feel fearful, so we always have our team take a few steps back to ensure we let the homeowner feel comfortable. But that comes with years of experience; so by documenting that level of detail, our new employees can skip the learning curve.

D: Test It With Someone

The last thing you want to do, after you've sketched it out and put it on a live document, is walk through the whole SOP with someone. Interestingly, not only does it help to walk through the document with your top technicians—maybe they do something you don't do that's really helpful—but it can also be helpful to walk through your SOP with someone who has *no idea* how it works.

For instance, when I'm creating SOPs at Albiware, my software company, I'll often ask my assistant to walk through it with me. She'll speak up if something doesn't quite make sense—this is really helpful because if I'm writing an Albiware Sales SOP, for instance, my assistant is coming at it with zero experience, and she's willing to ask all the questions, and that's exactly the level of detail I want in the SOP—I want to make sure I have every possible question answered, even for someone with no experience.

E: Use the 80-20 Rule

As a leader, it's your job to think outside the box, but your team's job is to problem solve from within the box (well, at least 80 percent of the time). Here is my rule of thumb for "freedom within the framework":

80 percent is copy & paste, and 20 percent is customizable.

SOPs aren't created for your benefit, but for that of your team. As we previously discussed, entrepreneurs often thrive in chaotic environments, but most of your employees do not. You want your SOPs to include 80 percent of their total job function, so that when the remaining 20 percent arises (unpredictable situations, outliers, etc.), they will have the confidence of the other 80 percent backing their decision.

Buy People Who Come With SOPs

SOPs are one of the most underrated elements in all of business. Try it—pick one area of your business that's creating a ton of headaches, and just take the time out to create an SOP right now.

A great place to start is with your job-flow SOP... start at the beginning, and walk through the whole thing...

How does the call come in? Who goes out to meet them? How do they sign a client? How do they finish the work? How do they bill for it…?

Now, if that sounds like a lot of work, I get it. Honestly, I've learned not to just build SOPs, but *buy* them. And I do that by *hiring* the right people—I can find someone who's already been there, done that, got the SOP, and ask them, "Hey, can you write an SOP for how to care for our $500,000 worth of restoration equipment?" At Albiware, I can hire a marketing director and ask them, "What's the playbook for marketing software to niche clientele? How do we start a marketing campaign? What are the steps? How much should it cost? What's our expected ROI?"

And then, I take that playbook, turn it into our SOP, and customize it, just a tad for our company.

So, you can just hire the people who come "preloaded" with the knowledge, the experience, and the training, then ask them to develop the SOP (because it's already in their mind).

Here's a Done-for-You SOP!

On that note, *I* have an SOP for you for water mitigation. This is the whole job flow, from when the call comes in, to when we get the check. It's in the back of the book, and feel free to copy it, past it, and tweak it, just about 20 percent for your company.

Head to the back of the book, or go to:
RestorationMillionaire.com/resources to find that SOP, and others (we add more for restoration all the time!).

Roadblocks

Maintaining an SOP is like going to the gym: go four to five days a week, eat x amount of calories, get x hours of sleep, etc. It can seem unnerving and even impossible at first to qualify which factors are important and what areas need more attention than others. But that is everyone's first mistake–they overcomplicate the process.

Bottom line, the odds are in your favor. Consistency will *always* beat complexity, and in a similar fashion, if you make the work *less* complicated, you'll experience less roadblocks. Here is an example of how we simplified our SOP through modifying our business practice:

If you're in restoration, you are familiar with the industry standard for "moisture checks." These daily visits ensure 1) the carpets dry properly and 2) the insurance companies receive logged accounts of how the equipment is being utilized while rented.

90 percent of the time, the carpet isn't dry until the 3rd or 4th day, so we asked ourselves, "why would we visit the location every day? To ensure it's still damp?" Checking on these houses every day was a waste of time and resources, and each house call was tedious to plan.

Insurance covers 3-4 days *anyway*, so we stopped wasting time and labor, and went to the property on the 4th day to complete the moisture check. This refusal to comply with unnecessarily complicated SOPs enabled our business to grow that much faster. Instead of technicians going from house to house, making sure the carpets dried, they were speaking to insurance companies, acquiring more jobs, and ultimately increasing our revenue.

The key takeaway is this: SOPs do not only provide the answer to a question, but they are also the solution to the question. Your SOPs should not be an index for how to respond to every problem, rather they need to be living frameworks which create consistent outcomes, higher performance from your team, and increased opportunities for your business to grow.

Momentum Trigger

Head to RestorationMillionaire.com/resources, or go to the back of the book and use the SOP there for water mitigation.

Or, if you aren't into water mitigation, take our SOP and build out your own, using this one as a guide.

Restorer's Recap

- SOPs will help you stay away from the Reactive Rollercoaster™: they'll make you feel peace, and create consistency, accountability, and predictability in your restoration business.
- The three main areas that restoration companies should create their SOPs in are:
    1) Job Flow
    2) Sales & Marketing
    3) Employee Onboarding
- To create an SOP, start by simply drawing it out "on the back of a napkin" style: create boxes and write in "step one: knock on the customer's door. Step two: Take three steps out." Then connect these boxes and label them, 1, 2, 3, etc.
- Once you have the basic ideas drawn out, ask someone on your team (perhaps your assistant) to put them into a *live*, editable, electronic version for your whole team.
- You can copy most SOPs from other, similar companies by at least 80 percent, then, customize them by 20 percent.

CHAPTER 9:
Crush the Referral Game... The *Right* Way

Fishing Hole II: *Add 1 Referral Source, $1-3 Million*
Fishing Hole III: *Add ALL Referral Sources, $3-5 Million*

New Tool

In this chapter, you're going to learn about Fishing Holes II and III—which means, we're going to be talking all about how to get from $1 million in revenue to $5 million in revenue.

Specifically, we're going to learn about a referral process I've developed called CIRCLS, which is the referral process I use as a part of the Restoration Millionaire Method™.

You can use CIRCLS to build *any* new referral partnership:

C-I-R-C-L-S

Connect: Think of the people you want to *create connections with* or need to build relationships with. In our case, it was the insurance agents.

Identify: Find what's *important to who you want to connect with.* In this scenario, what was important to insurance agents was renewals.

Relieve: Solve a big pain point *of theirs.* Insurance agents were tired of dealing with claims (something they know almost *nothing* about, because they're salespeople).

Craft: Re-imagine your product as something that matters *to them.* In our case, we didn't have to come up with a new product. We simply remarketed what we wanted anyway (which was to meet the homeowners) as a "claims screening process."

Loop: Close the loop by shining the light back on them. We made sure to tell every homeowner that they only received this special claims-screening process because they had their insurance agent.

Systemize: Have a *system* setup that allows you to build the relationships like clockwork.

My dad was a fantastic business partner at Romexterra. And, we'd found a *fantastic* marketing partner for our online ads. By the time Romexterra was two years old, we were spending ten grand a month on online marketing, and we couldn't believe it... but we were already doing about $3 million in revenue *after only two years.*

I was a young gunner—remember, I'm all *Jack*—so I thought, *Hey, let's just triple our marketing budget, and we'll triple our revenue, right?*

Well... Alex was *not* so right.

By then, our fantastic marketing partner was helping us close about $70,000 a month in business with $10,000 in digital ads, on Google, Bing, social media, etc.

So, I increased our marketing budget with them to $30,000. If our CAC[22] had stayed the same, that means that our new marketing budget

---

[22] Customer acquisition cost

should have made us about $210,000 a month in work. But instead, by tripling our marketing budget,.. we made exactly the same amount of new work.

Not my proudest moment, but I remember getting really, *really* frustrated with our marketing team. After waiting a few months and seeing no more results, I'd finally had enough, and I took it out on our marketing partner. He was a great guy, and he really listened to me (even though I was in a huff). Then, he told me something that was pretty shocking:

"Alex, I think you've hit the point of diminishing returns."[23]

What the Heck Are "Diminishing Returns"?

In chapter three, we talked about the Restoration Millionaire Method™. There, you learned all about Fishing Hole I: online marketing.

That single Fishing Hole should get you all the way to $1 million. But eventually, just like I did, you'll hit a certain point when that Fishing Hole will no longer add any more value. That point is called *diminishing returns.*

Diminishing returns is a bit of a technical term. Basically, diminishing returns is the point at which something that once worked great will yield no more fruit even with increased pressure. So, for instance, when you first learn a new task, say, how to write a poem, it may take you a day. After a lot of practice, you may be able to do it in an hour. But, at some point it won't matter how much harder you try or how much more you practice, you just won't be able to do it any faster.

Or, think of buying things in bulk. If you buy a toothbrush, it may cost you $3. If you buy two toothbrushes in a pack, maybe each one costs you $2. If you buy *five* in a pack, it may only cost you $1 each. But, at

---

[23] Diminishing returns is a point at which something that was once working really well, starts generating less and less returns.

some point, you won't save much more money by buying fifteen or twenty toothbrushes—that's because you hit the point of diminishing returns.

And that's what happens in marketing, and that's a great sign that it is time to move to a new Fishing Hole.

At Romexterra, we hit our point of diminishing returns with online marketing at $3 million in revenue. Online marketing had helped us to get to that point, but if I kept investing in it... we'd still be at $3 million in revenue. So, thankfully, I listened to our marketing partner, because it was finally time to find a new Fishing Hole...

Your Next 2 Fishing Holes

In this chapter, we're going to discuss how to first go from just online marketing (Fishing Hole I) to adding *one* additional referral source (Fishing Hole II). I'll give you a specific system that you can use for whichever referral source you like.

Once you've maximized that referral source, you then add on every possible referral source, keeping everything else in your business the same—online marketing, one service, your original referral source. That will be Fishing Hole III.

So, you'll find how to go from one Fishing Hole to three Fishing Holes in this one chapter, and the tool you're going to use is called CIRCLS, which we'll discuss later.

But before we get into *how* to do referrals, let's talk about how *not* to do them.

How *Not* to Plumb for Referrals

When it's time to move to a new Fishing Hole, you'll want to find one that offers the same return. While we didn't exactly know what to do and we tried a lot of different things—no one had offered us the Restoration Millionaire Method™—we *ended up* doing referrals really, really well.

The reason I put referrals as stop number-two on the Restoration Millionaire Method™, is because you can start from nowhere with online marketing, and it's pretty easy to generate some business. Now, after you've been in the community for a while, you'll have a bit of a name for yourself, and you'll know a little better how things go. In fact, after you've made your first $1 million with online marketing, you'll already have made some connections with insurance agents, plumbers, builders, and others in the industry—you're probably *already* doing referral work, without even knowing it!

While you may be tempted to add on more services—or you may have already—I still say to focus on *one service.* If you're doing mitigation work, do mitigation work. If you're doing reconstruction, do reconstruction. Don't branch out beyond that *one* service you offer, even after you've maximized online marketing. Because referrals are a much easier way to get to $5 million quickly.

***

Now, at this stage, when it's time to create referral partners in the industry, let me tell you how *not* to do it.

Another restoration company within our Chicagoland market was marketing to plumbers with a 15-percent *cash* commission rate. They went straight to plumbers and offered them a 15 percent cut (in *cash!)* of any rebuild or restoration work the plumber would send them. When a plumber shows up at a customer's home to fix a plumbing issue, they often find that a wall, a floor, or something else needs to be repaired which is outside a plumber's skill. So, they'll recommend another company, like a restoration company, to a homeowner. The restoration company will often give a small kickback to plumbers as a thank-you.

But 15 percent, in *cash*? No way. Something didn't "smell right," you know what I mean? At Romexterra, we knew we couldn't compete with that. And, in fact, it wasn't only the money our competitor was giving away—they held plumber parties at casinos, had motorcycle giveaways for plumbers... basically, they dangled any carrot they could in front of the local plumbers. (I used to call them "plumber sluts." Fondly, of course.)

So, that was *one* way to build referrals. Instead, though, we looked elsewhere. And we found a perfect plan within the insurance agents.

Our "Claims Screening Process"

I'm not the first restorer by any means to talk about making connections within the insurance world. In fact, as you know, that's where restorers get a ton of their work. First, let me say, I don't really talk much about TPAs, because that involves getting "in bed" with the insurance companies in a very close way. To me that creates a bit of a conflict of interest when it comes to the homeowner—the insurance company wants to pay as little as possible, even if that's not in the best interest of the homeowner.

But it's another matter entirely to become friends with the insurance *agents.* And this is where the magic can really happen. You see, the insurance agents get more work pushed to them than anyone else, because, when Mr. Homeowner has a problem with his home, such as a leak, a fire, or what he thinks may be wind damage, he often calls his agent. So, smart restorers think *Gee, wouldn't it be great if Mr. Agent called* me *before they called another restorer?*

Well, that's what all the other restorers were doing. So, when my father and I maxed out online marketing, we thought, *Well, let's do what everyone else is doing!* So, we started doing what most of the other trades people do... sending donuts to insurance agents, and we even offered to wine and dine each of them, just like all the other restorers. And that's what we did for a couple months—we wined and dined, and dropped off donuts and pens, and we bragged—just like all the other stories—about our A+ BBB[24] rating. But you know what?

The insurance agent couldn't care less about our triple alphabetized rating. It doesn't matter to them. That's because *the insurance agent* isn't a restorer, a contractor, or a builder. In fact, oddly, even though they're

---

[24] Better Business Bureau

the first person homeowners call, insurance agents don't actually know anything about claims, at all: They don't know about drying carpets, rebuilding walls, how fire damage works, removing smoke from clothes, none of it. They know one thing really well:

Selling insurance policies.

Because selling *policies* and policy renewals are how insurance agents make their money—they're paid a commission on policies and renewal.

So, while my father and I had correctly found that referrals would be our next stop to making millions in restoration, we hadn't quite cracked the code of our referral program. But after we realized that wining and dining and donuts were doing nothing, we hatched a new plan, one that worked like a charm.

After I did a little research to find out what insurance agents *do* care about (policy renewals), I found out something interesting: the number-one reason customers leave their insurance company, and an agent loses their renewal commission, is because of a poor claims experience. That's right, here's a little interesting tidbit:

Policy increases are *not* why people leave insurance companies; it's because they try to make a claim, and they hate the experience, so, they leave and find a new company.

And that was our *in* with the agents. I decided that I'd help solve *the agent's* problem—bad claims experience.

Interestingly, at Romexterra, we didn't even have to change anything about what we did. I just had to rebrand a service that we (and, truthfully, every other restoration company) already has to do—which is find out if a homeowner's issue is actually insurable, meaning, "Will the insurance company pay for this?"

That's something every restorer has to determine during every sale to a homeowner, so, you and I know a *lot* more than an insurance agent about whether a claim is insurable. So, that's what I started telling the insurance agents: we told them that we offered a new "claims-screening service."

We explained it like this:

"Mr. Agent, you probably already know this, but the top reason people don't renew their insurance policies is because of poor claims experiences. That's why, here at our restoration company, we offer a service called a "claims-screening service." Here's how it works: When a homeowner calls you, you can call us and ask *us* to go out to the house and take a look at the leak, the supposed hail damage, or whatever the problem is. Then, we'll let you and the homeowner know our opinion on whether it's insurable or not (you see, we see this kind of thing all the time, so we really know what to look for.) A lot of the times, homeowners just need some reassurance, and they don't really have a claim. Let's say your homeowner just has a leaky faucet or something we can fix—often, we can fix that for *free* for your homeowner, and we'll even let them know we provided that free service because they work with *you.* If for some reason there is an insurable claim, we'll let you know that, too. You'll never have to go out to the home, and we'll keep you in the loop with everything."

I bet you can only imagine how that really set the table for a great relationship with the local insurance agents! They *loved it!*

We were solving *their* pain point—bad claims experience, which led to lack of renewals, meaning less commission checks in the agents' pockets.

Once we started telling insurance agents we'd go to their policyholders' homes *for free* to screen claims, our phone wouldn't stop ringing.

The cool thing is, this service also provided a huge win for homeowners. Because, many of them would open claims for fairly petty problems and then, later, they wouldn't get money from the insurance company, and then, they'd have a claim on their account, making their policy potentially go up. By screening their issue first, we made sure they weren't wasting a claim on something that dinged their account unnecessarily. On the flip side, if they actually had a real issue to claim, we made sure to fix it with expertise.

So, we started taking more and more calls. Sure, we did take on some extra petty work—and fixed some free squeaky doors and leaky faucets for free—but we started getting tons of great work through these referrals every time we did find a legitimate claim.

Also, we made sure to close the loop with homeowners, directing them *back* to the agents, so everyone was happy, and the referrals kept flowing:

"Hey Mrs. Homeowner, we took a look, and here's what we think... I'm so glad we were able to help you so quickly and efficiently, and that only happened because you use your insurance agent, who has great connections with us. Remember that when it's time to renew your policy!"

Think about how that made the insurance agent feel!

This referral program *worked like a charm.* Agents routed homeowners straight to us, we solved problems and built relationships with the homeowners, and pointed them back to their insurance agents, who kept feeding us more claims to screen. Everyone won! We became the go-to claims-screeners, giving us a two-way "in" with both the insurance agents and the homeowners.

Fishing Hole II: Add 1 Referral Source

To be clear, the point of Fishing Hole II is *not* "create a claims screening process," but rather "add *one* referral source."

While insurance agents are a fantastic avenue, there are probably several other avenues you have access to—maybe developing relationships with other restorers who have niched down on different services, or even other trades people, such as roofers, plumbers, or others who have different specialties and can give you work.

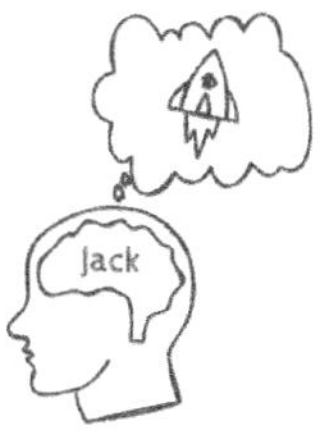

Jacks, this should be easy for you. You're probably already talking and building relationships with people who can refer others to you. Georges, you may have to go out of our comfort zone a bit, but you can do this.

Those are all great sources and, the point of Fishing Hole II is to pick *one.*

Just as we tell you to fish from one hole at a time, the same thing applies, here. Find one referral source that you can spend your time and energy on, and develop it fully. That referral source should easily take you to $3 million. Then, once you've really figured out how to do referrals, you can move on to Fishing Hole III, which is to keep your *one* service and attack *every referral source you can!*

So, you need a plan, a way to go after referrals. You can follow the same sort of guide that enabled us to build great relationships with our agents. The good news is you can use this with whatever referral source you decide to use.

C-I-R-C-L-S

The plan is simple, and it's called CIRCLS:

Connect: Think of the people you want to *create connections with* or need to build relationships with. In our case, it was the insurance agents.

Identify: Find what's *important to who you want to connect with.* In this scenario, what was important to insurance agents was renewals.

Relieve: Solve a big pain point *of theirs.* Insurance agents were tired of dealing with claims (something they know almost *nothing* about, because they're salespeople).

Craft: Re-imagine your product as something that matters *to them.* In our case, we didn't have to come up with a new product. We simply remarketed what we wanted anyway (which was to meet the homeowners) as a "claims screening process."

Loop: Close the loop by shining the light back on them. We made sure to tell every homeowner that they only received this special claims-screening process because they had their insurance agent.

Systemize: Have a *system* setup that allows you to build the relationships like clockwork.

Did you notice the "s" at the end? This is one area I ended up adding on *later,* because it took a while to figure out. But what we ended up doing was having someone in charge of these insurance agent relationships, and their role was pretty simple: talk to fifteen agents a day, five days a week, on a four-week rotation. In this way, each person we hired to talk to our insurance-agent partners would speak with 300 agents every month! Then, they'd start the next month back on the four-week rotation. So, it works like this: If Lindsey was in charge of insurance agent relationships, she'd go online and download a list of 300 insurance agents in our area. Then, she'd talk to fifteen of them every day during the week. By the end of the month, she would have spoken with all of them, and she'd start back over at the beginning of the month, that way every agent was touched monthly, which is a good amount, but not so much to where you're annoying.

You can use this same CIRCLS process with *anyone* to build referrals. Not only did we do it with the insurance agents, but we looked elsewhere, and we did it with firefighters as well.

As firefighters are often the heroes who show up first in a homeowner's life, we wanted to build tightknit relationships with all our firefighting heroes in Chicagoland. So, we applied the same principles as we had done with the insurance agents.

First, we wanted to *connect* with them, so we *identified* what was most important to them. We discovered, pretty easily, that firefighters care most about their communities. They take on modest incomes in exchange for breathing in carcinogenic air and running into burning buildings because they really love the people in their areas. After identifying this, we made sure to *relieve* a specific pain point for these heroes. To show these firefighters that we were legitimate companies who would be around for the long haul and weren't going to scam their communities, we *crafted* a few free services for their communities. Here's what we did: We offered a couple free packages to homeowners. One, we called "victim assistance," and we would come in and clean the furniture, take their pets on a walk, help determine what personal belongings were salvageable, and a few other things. Secondly, we also offered "board-ups" for homeowners that needed to board up their home after a disaster who didn't have insurance or the funds to pay for the services. By offering these two free services to the community, we were investing in what was important to our firefighters. We made sure to let the firefighters know that we'd offer those services *without being pushy,* in any way, to homeowners, and that they could take advantage of those services whether or not they wanted to work with us. The firefighters were then *thrilled* to suggest these services to homeowners. Later, as we developed better relationships with the chiefs and others, they invited us to fundraising events, 9/11 workouts that honored victims of the September 11 attacks, and, during COVID, we even conducted free COVID cleanups for fire stations in our area, as our way of giving back to the community. In this way, we honored them in front of the community of homeowners that they served (*loop*). The final "s" (systemize) was that we had an office person who was officially in charge of keeping up with all the fire stations' fundraising and other events, so that way we never missed one.

With these firefighters, we were utilizing the same CIRCLS method.

Note: At Albi, we have a customer relationship management software (or CRM) that helps you implement CIRCLS on a systematic, planned, basis, without all the hassle! Go check it out at Albiware.com, where you can sign up for a free demo—trust me, putting in an organized, systematic referral program can quickly add millions in revenue to your business!

Fishing Hole III: Add ALL Referral Sources

So, the first step is to determine which *one* referral source you want to use. There's quite a few:

- Other tradesmen
- TPAs[25]
- Insurance agents
- Firefighters
- Others

First, choose *one* referral source, and keep your internet marketing going, and stick with the one service that you've been providing.

Build up your own referral source, continuing to improve upon the system until it runs like clockwork. That one referral source, with continued online marketing, should get you to $3 million, fairly easily.

From there, you simply take everything you've learned about referrals, and you duplicate it to *all* referral sources, using Set, Prove, Rep.

Blended CAC

The important thing as you move from one Fishing Hole to the next, is to *keep the CAC as low as possible.*

Earlier, when we discussed Fishing Hole #1: online marketing, we talked about keeping the CAC to about 10 to 20 percent. Importantly, you only add your first referral source when you've hit the point of diminishing returns with online marketing (remember how I couldn't harvest any more work from online marketing, no matter how much more I invested?). Once you decide it's time to add on your first referral source, you'll need to consider your CAC, and compare it to what it was

---

[25] Although, I really don't suggest these.

previously, knowing that, at first, it *will definitely* increase, and, in the end *it may also increase.*

It may take a while to ensure you know how to do referrals, and in the meantime you may accidentally waste money (although you don't need to do it as absurdly as our friends the "plumber sluts"!). So, let's assume that your CAC from online marketing (Fishing Hole I) is 15 percent. That will be your target when you add on your first referral source, at least after ninety days. Let's say your first two months your CAC jumps as you try to get the hang of your referral sources and who to pay to do what. But then, after a few months, your new CAC is 20 percent for Fishing Hole II.

So, now, your online marketing CAC is 15 percent, and your referral CAC is 20 percent. If you generated the same revenue on both, *your blended* CAC would be 17.5 percent. Yes, I know, *blended CAC* is a new term, but it's actually pretty easy to calculate. You just divide the total marketing dollars you spent by the total work that all your marketing brought in, and that's your blended CAC:

Blended CAC: Total spent on all marketing ÷ total made from all marketing.

Keep Crushing It

If you follow CIRCLS to add one referral source, then, once you've implemented one fantastic referral system, you can add *all* referral sources.

Once you've done both of these, you'll be well on your way to $5 million in revenue... and pretty soon, it will be time to go on.

Momentum Trigger

Almost no restorer I've worked with has truly systemized their referral sources as well as they could. So, whether you've already added referral sources to your Fishing Holes yet or not, I have the same suggestion: identify the one referral source that has the most ROI, and then, from there, implement CIRCLS to truly systemize that referral source.

As always, you can go to RestorationMillionaire.com/resources to get some assistance crushing that first referral source.

Restorer's Recap

- **Fishing Hole II: Add 1 Referral Source to $3 million.** After you've made your first million utilizing online marketing, it's time to move on to Fishing Hole II: add one referral source. Importantly, the Restoration Millionaire Method™ suggests that you *do not* add more services until you've maximized all referral sources.
- **Use CIRCLS to truly systemize the way you're running referral programs:**

    Connect: Think of the people you want to *create connections with* or need to build relationships with. In our case, it was the insurance agents. **Identify:** Find what's *important to who you want to connect with.* In this scenario, what was important to insurance agents was renewals.

    Identify: Find what's *important to who you want to connect with.* In this scenario, what was important to insurance agents was renewals.

    Relieve: Solve a big pain point *of theirs.* Insurance agents were tired of dealing with claims (something they know almost *nothing* about, because they're salespeople).

    Craft: Re-imagine your product as something that matters *to them.* In our case, we didn't have to come up with a new product. We simply remarketed what we wanted anyway (which was to meet the homeowners) as a "claims screening process."

    Loop: Close the loop by shining the light back on them. We made sure to tell every homeowner that they only received this special claims-screening process because they had their insurance agent.

    Systemize: Have a *system* setup that allows you to build the relationships like clockwork.

- **Fishing Hole III: Add ALL referral sources to $5 million.** Once you've successfully executed, systemized, and easily ran one referral program for one referral source, take what you've learned, and expand it to *every referral source.*
- **Blended CAC:** This is the calculation of *all marketing dollars* divided by *all work received* from all marketing sources. So, in one month, you spent $10,000 on online marketing and $10,000 on your referral programs, then made $50,000 from online marketing and $40,000 from referrals, then your blended CAC would be $20,000 ÷$90,000 = 22 percent.

CHAPTER 10:
Call Your Shots... With Metrics

"If you can't measure it, you can't improve it."
—Peter Drucker[26]

New Tool

In this chapter, we're going to learn about the Restoration Scorecard™, which you can find online at: RestorationMillionaire.com/resources, but here's a screenshot of *part* of one here:

Found on your P&L

COMPANYWIDE METRICS		Month of January				
		Jan 1-2	Jan 3-9	Jan 10-16	Jan 17-23	Jan 24-30
REVENUE						
Invoicing	Service #1					
	Service #2					
	Service #3					
	Service #4					
	Total	0	0	0	0	0
COGS	Service #1					
	Service #2					
	Service #3					
	Service #4					
	Total	0	0	0	0	0
Gross Margin	Service #1					
	Service #2					
	Service #3					
	Service #4					
	Total	0	0	0	0	0
WIP	Service #1					
	Service #2					
	Service #3					
	Service #4					
	Total Work In Progress	0	0	0	0	0

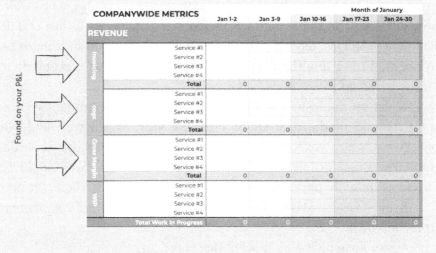

[26] Drucker, Peter Ferdinand. 1967. *The Effective Executive.* New York : Harper & Row.

If you're on a plane from New York to Los Angeles, you'd expect your pilot to take the most direct route, right?

But what if, as you sit down, put your bag beneath the chair in front of you and click your seat belt, you hear the overhead intercom:

Hey folks, thanks for choosing Duta Airlines! Hope y'all are ready for the scenic route today. Sit tight for an extra four hours of flight time and enjoy the view. For any inconvenience, extra snacks and drinks will be available upon request from our amazing flight attendants. Again, thanks for flying Duta Airlines.

This scenario seems absurd, right? Who would possibly want to voluntarily sit on a flight for an extra four hours?

While the absurdity is a bit obvious in the context of a flight, I've seen dozens of entrepreneurs choose the "scenic" option for their business trip, time and time again.

Far too often, business owners wait until the end of the year to check their financial statements, their profit-and-loss statements, or other important metrics of the business. Particularly in restoration, when we're very vulnerable to the Reactive Rollercoaster™, many of us just end up handling problems, day after day, reacting to what's right in front of us, as opposed to setting the flight path, and then checking in regularly to ensure we're on it.

When we could be checking our sales numbers monthly, we wait until the end of the quarter, or even the year. When we should be checking out how we're doing on our turn-on-receivables, we never do, until it's a real problem and cashflow is low. When we should be checking in with our work-in-progress to find out if there are any speedbumps we can avoid, we just shrug, *No customers are complaining at the moment.*

Again, imagine if a pilot acted that way?

A flight from New York to L.A. *should* take six hours. To execute on that timeline, experienced pilots are trained to check their heading and course-correct every few minutes. Minor adjustments, again and again, that keep the plane flying in what looks like a relatively straight line.

But what if a pilot only checked the wind speed, heading, and other instrumentation only every hour? That six-hour flight could easily turn in to eight hours or more.

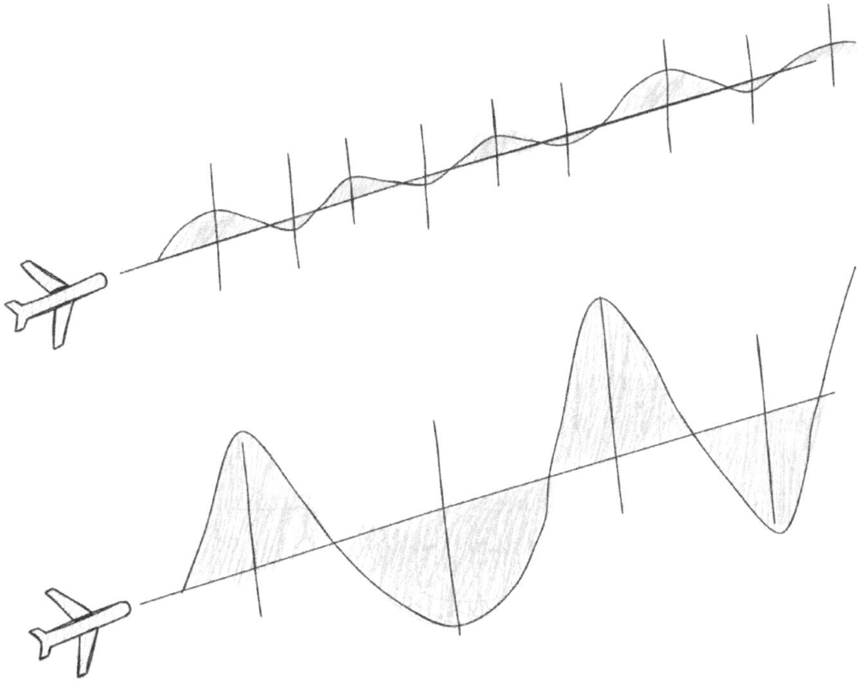

Pilots know that to stay on the most direct path to their destination, the have to check everything, constantly, on a regular cadence to make minor corrections. This sort of regular check-ins not only ensures the most direct path, but also helps eliminate potentially stressful navigational scenarios, where one gets far off course, and ends up in an unanticipated storm, in the wrong flight path, or flying in a no-fly zone.

And that's what we're going to discuss in this chapter—how to set a goal and make repeated adjustments to our journey throughout our business throughout the year, so that we never end up too far off course.

After coaching countless restoration and home service owners, I figured it out: people don't understand how predictable the restoration business can be. You really can be a Proactive Pilot. Excuses like "sales just aren't good right now" or "there just aren't any good technicians out there anymore" are what will take you from a six-hour flight to a ten-hour one.

Take the Quickest Flight Path

In the early years at Romexterra, we didn't really have *any* checkups on how our business was performing—we didn't know our sales numbers, our accounts receivables (or even what that was!) or net income. After a year, we put in some basic protocols, such as checking up on our quarterly profit-and-loss statements. But it wasn't until we realized the importance of reviewing our numbers consistently did we feel totally in control of the company.

Eventually, we put in *weekly* measurements, using a report called a Flash Report. Each week, my father and I would sit down and review a list of metrics, from cost-of-goods sold, to work-in-progress, to qualified leads. It didn't take long until we were solving problems faster and avoiding major headaches. We ended that first year of tracking our flash reports doing very well.

By the end of our *second* year tracking our weekly metrics, we were at $6 million in revenue, and landed within *1 percent* of our beginning of year prediction! That's the power of putting in a regular cadence of going over basic metrics. You can land *right* where you should.

***

In this chapter, we're going to use a basic scorecard similar to the flash report my father and I used. It's called the Restoration Scorecard™. You may have heard about scorecards, reports, or reviews for other businesses. Similar in purpose, the Restoration Scorecard™ is designed specifically for restoration owners to take control of their business. This tool suits businesses of all sizes, meaning you can start using this tomorrow and immediately see where your business needs help.

It is most beneficial when updated and reviewed on a weekly basis. If you don't already, set weekly meetings to go over your business's performance with your top leaders so each member of the team is equally aware of the company's progress. Each review, you'll see your actuals versus your projections, giving you a side-by-side comparison of your current performance and how far you have left to go.

On the next two pages, you can see a full breakdown of what ours looks like. We keep it in one Google Sheet:

COMPANYWIDE METRICS		Month of January										
		Jan 1-2	Jan 3-9	Jan 10-16	Jan 17-23	Jan 24-30	Jan 31	Jan Actuals	Jan Goals	Feb 1-6	Feb 7-13	Feb 14
REVENUE												
Invoicing	Service #1							0				
	Service #2							0				
	Service #3							0				
	Service #4							0				
	Total	0	0	0	0	0	0	0		0	0	
COGS	Service #1							0				
	Service #2							0				
	Service #3							0				
	Service #4							0				
	Total	0	0	0	0	0	0	0		0	0	
Gross Margin	Service #1							0				
	Service #2							0				
	Service #3							0				
	Service #4							0				
	Total	0	0	0	0	0	0	0		0	0	
WIP	Service #1							0				
	Service #2							0				
	Service #3							0				
	Service #4							0				
	Total Work In Progress	0	0	0	0	0	0	0		0	0	
SALES & MARKETING												
Qualified Opportunities	Referral Source #1							0				
	Referral Source #2							0				
	Referral Source #3							0				
	Referral Source #4							0				
	Total	0	0	0	0	0	0	0		0	0	
Estimated Revenue	Referral Source #1							0				
	Referral Source #2							0				
	Referral Source #3							0				
	Referral Source #4							0				
	Total	0	0	0	0	0	0	0		0	0	
Won Opportunities	Referral Source #1							0				
	Referral Source #2							0				
	Referral Source #3							0				
	Referral Source #4							0				
	Total	0	0	0	0	0	0	0		0	0	
Closing Rate	Referral Source #1							0				
	Referral Source #2							0				
	Referral Source #3							0				
	Referral Source #4							0				
	Closing Rate:	#DIV/0!	#DIV/0!	#DIV/0!	#DIV/0!	#DIV/0!	#DIV/0!	#DIV/0!		#DIV/0!	#DIV/0!	#DIV/
	Marketing Expenses:							0				
Financials												
	90 Day Average Monthly Sales	1600000										
	Accounts Receivable	6400000						6400000				
	Turn On Receivable	121.6666667	#DIV/0!	#DIV/0!	#DIV/0!	#DIV/0!	#DIV/0!	#DIV/0!		#DIV/0!	#DIV/0!	#DIV/
CashFlow	Accounts Payable							#DIV/0!				
	Next Payroll							0				
	Cash In							0				
	Cash Out							0				
	Cash on Hand							0				
	Lines of Credit											
	Total Limit On Lines of Credit							#DIV/0!				
	Balance Due on the Lines of Credit							#DIV/0!				
	Total Cash Available							#DIV/0!				
Production												
Operations	Number of Production Employees							#DIV/0!				
	Weekly Production Payroll Hours							#DIV/0!				
	Average Hourly Week							#DIV/0!				
	Estimate Lag (Days)							#DIV/0!				
	Invoice Lag (Days)							#DIV/0!				
	Revenue Per Production Employee	#DIV/0!	#DIV/0!	#DIV/0!	#DIV/0!	#DIV/0!	#DIV/0!	#DIV/0!		#DIV/0!	#DIV/0!	#DIV/

Get an editable version of this sheet at:
www.RestorationMillionaire.com/resources

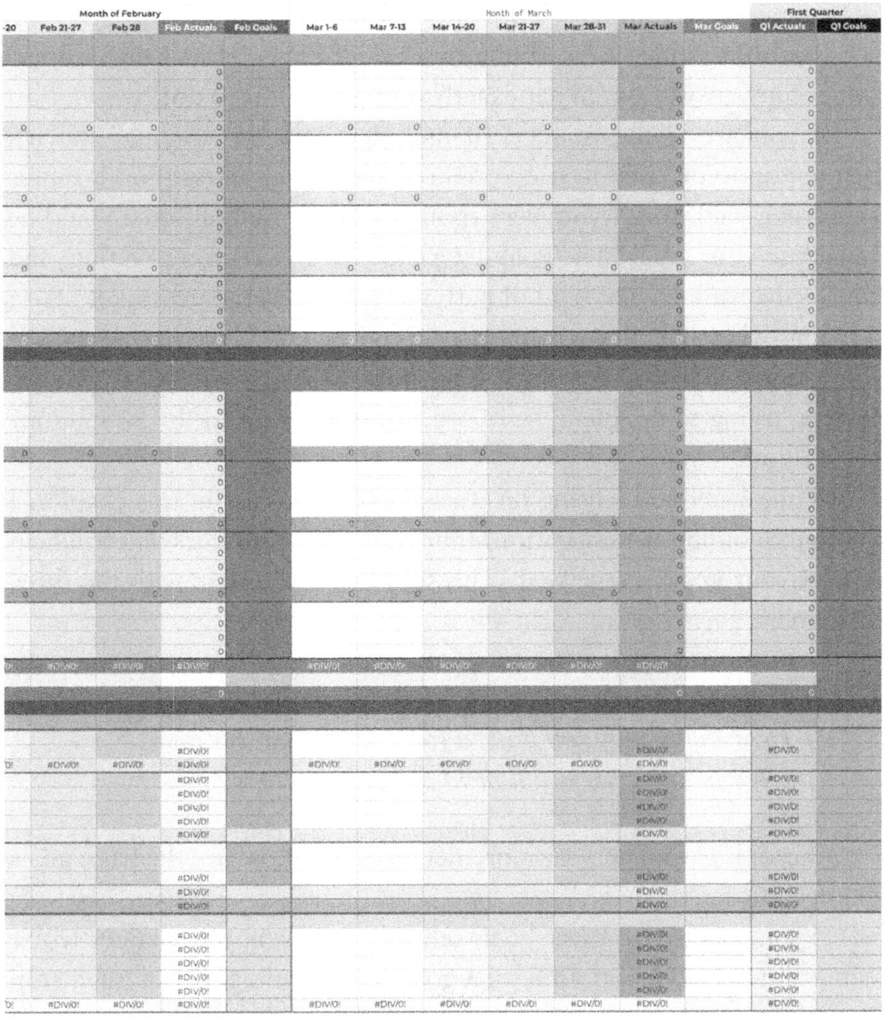

	Month of February						Month of March					First Quarter	
-20	Feb 21-27	Feb 28	Feb Actuals	Feb Goals	Mar 1-6	Mar 7-13	Mar 14-20	Mar 21-27	Mar 28-31	Mar Actuals	Mar Goals	Q1 Actuals	Q1 Goals
			0							0		0	
			0							0		0	
			0							0		0	
			0							0		0	
0	0	0	0		0	0	0	0	0	0		0	
			0							0		0	
			0							0		0	
			0							0		0	
			0							0		0	
0	0	0	0		0	0	0	0	0	0		0	
			0							0		0	
			0							0		0	
			0							0		0	
			0							0		0	
0	0	0	0		0	0	0	0	0	0		0	
			0							0		0	
			0							0		0	
			0							0		0	
			0							0		0	
0	0	0	0		0	0	0	0	0	0			
			0							0		0	
			0							0		0	
			0							0		0	
			0							0		0	
0	0	0	0		0	0	0	0	0	0		0	
			0							0		0	
			0							0		0	
			0							0		0	
			0							0		0	
0	0	0	0		0	0	0	0	0	0		0	
			0							0		0	
			0							0		0	
			0							0		0	
			0							0		0	
0	0	0	0		0	0	0	0	0	0		0	
			0							0		0	
			0							0		0	
			0							0		0	
			0							0		0	
0!	#DIV/0!	#DIV/0!	#DIV/0!		#DIV/0!	#DIV/0!	#DIV/0!	#DIV/0!	#DIV/0!	#DIV/0!			
			0							0		0	
			#DIV/0!							#DIV/0!		#DIV/0!	
0!	#DIV/0!	#DIV/0!	#DIV/0!		#DIV/0!	#DIV/0!	#DIV/0!	#DIV/0!	#DIV/0!	#DIV/0!			
			#DIV/0!							#DIV/0!		#DIV/0!	
			#DIV/0!							#DIV/0!		#DIV/0!	
			#DIV/0!							#DIV/0!		#DIV/0!	
			#DIV/0!							#DIV/0!		#DIV/0!	
			#DIV/0!							#DIV/0!		#DIV/0!	
			#DIV/0!							#DIV/0!		#DIV/0!	
			#DIV/0!							#DIV/0!		#DIV/0!	
			#DIV/0!							#DIV/0!		#DIV/0!	
			#DIV/0!							#DIV/0!		#DIV/0!	
			#DIV/0!							#DIV/0!		#DIV/0!	
			#DIV/0!							#DIV/0!		#DIV/0!	
			#DIV/0!							#DIV/0!		#DIV/0!	
			#DIV/0!							#DIV/0!		#DIV/0!	
0!	#DIV/0!	#DIV/0!	#DIV/0!		#DIV/0!	#DIV/0!	#DIV/0!	#DIV/0!	#DIV/0!	#DIV/0!		#DIV/0!	

First, What's Your Goal?

Restorers come to me all the time and ask me "How's my business doing?" my answer is: "What exactly do you want it to do?"

If you are trying to hit $10 million a year in revenue, and it's October and you only have $5 million, well, your restoration business isn't doing well. But if you were trying to hit $4 million, then you'd be exceeding your goals! The goal determines how well you're doing, and it helps determine what kind of path you need to set to get there.

This whole chapter will help show you exactly how your business is doing, but that's only helpful if you know how well you *want* it to do. Are you trying to double in size? Are you trying to grow by $1 million? $10 million?

While we'll be focusing on tracking your metrics in this chapter, I have a tool online at RestorationMillionaire.com/resources that will help you set your goal for the year. This tool helps you start with the three basic goals:

1) *Your end-of-year revenue goals*
2) *How many jobs you'll need to generate that revenue*
3) *How many leads you'll need to land that many jobs.*

Our online tool gets *far* more detailed, but those are the basic goals you need to set.

If you don't have those goals set, the metrics in this chapter won't matter much. So, if you do have a goal, keep reading. If not, then stop here, and first set the three goals above. (And check out our online tools to help you!)

The Restoration Scorecard™

You'll notice that there are four main sections:

- Revenue
- Sales & Marketing

- Financials
- Production

Then, within each of those sections, there are multiple metrics. Through years of iteration (Set, Prove, Rep, for the win!) my team has attempted to make this both as detailed as necessary while as simple as possible. You can go online and get a free template to make it your own at RestorationMillioniare.com/Resources

Section 1: Revenue

Section 1 is similar to your profit and loss statements. For each service you provide, you are able to keep track of a total "invoiced" amount, total "cost of goods sold," your "gross margin," and a super valuable category called "WIP: Work in Progress.

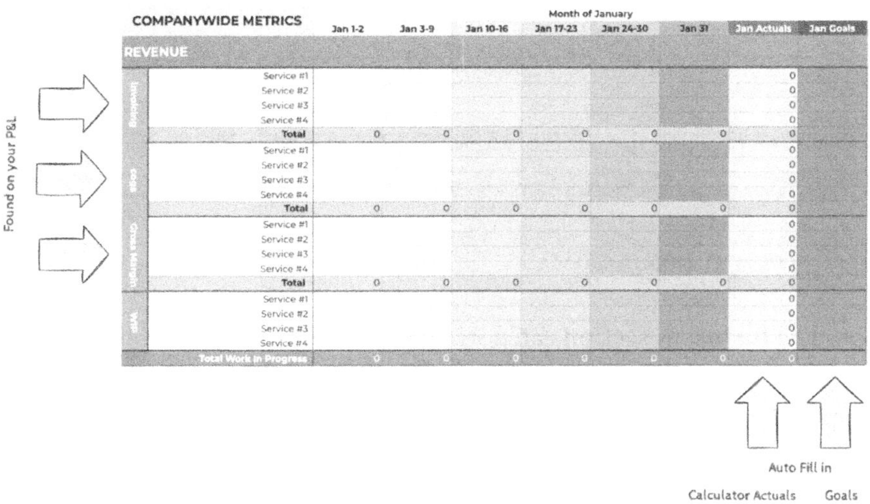

Tracking your WIPs are a great way to predict how much work you have yet to produce. This is a great way to see if you're off on your sales goal or not.

Section 2: Sales & Marketing

I use the sales & marketing section to understand how all our "Fishing Holes" are performing.

You can measure your "qualified opportunities," "estimated revenue," "won opportunities" (which can be determined differently, company to company), and "closing rate" (which can also be determined differently, company to company).

SALES & MARKETING								
Qualified Opportunities	Referral Source #1							0
	Referral Source #2							0
	Referral Source #3							0
	Referral Source #4							0
	Total	0	0	0	0	0	0	0
Estimated Revenue	Referral Source #1							0
	Referral Source #2							0
	Referral Source #3							0
	Referral Source #4							0
	Total	0	0	0	0	0	0	0
Won Opportunities	Referral Source #1							0
	Referral Source #2							0
	Referral Source #3							0
	Referral Source #4							0
	Total	0	0	0	0	0	0	0
Closing Rate	Referral Source #1							0
	Referral Source #2							0
	Referral Source #3							0
	Referral Source #4							0
	Closing Rate:	#DIV/0!	#DIV/0!	#DIV/0!	#DIV/0!	#DIV/0!	#DIV/0!	#DIV/0!
	Marketing Expenses:							0

Section 3: Financials

The financials section categorizes your cash flow. Importantly, here, you'll find your "turn on receivables," which we discussed at the end of chapter four.

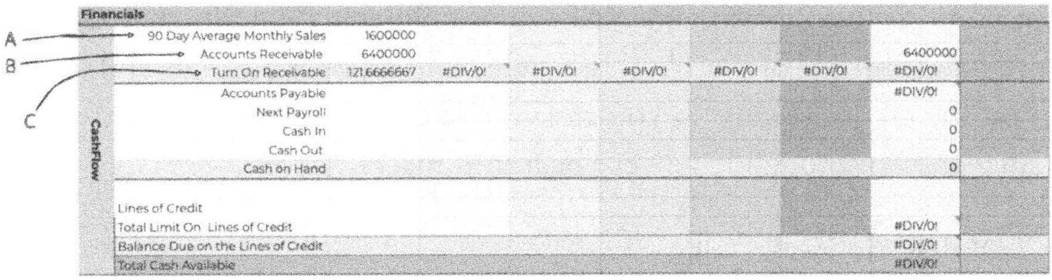

90 Day Average Monthly Sales	1600000						
Accounts Receivable	6400000						6400000
Turn On Receivable	121.6666667	#DIV/0!	#DIV/0!	#DIV/0!	#DIV/0!	#DIV/0!	#DIV/0!
Accounts Payable							#DIV/0!
Next Payroll							0
Cash In							0
Cash Out							0
Cash on Hand							0
Lines of Credit							
Total Limit On Lines of Credit							#DIV/0!
Balance Due on the Lines of Credit							#DIV/0!
Total Cash Available							#DIV/0!

(B/A) x 30 = C (Accounts Receivable/90-Day Avg Sales) x 30 = Turn on Receivables

Again, the calculation is as follows:[27]

(Total Accounts receivable / 90-day average monthly sales) x 30

Other crucial metrics include "accounts payable" (how much you owe), "next payroll," "cash in/out," and "cash on hand."

Section 4: Production

Production metrics measure the performance of your operational systems. Categories include "number of production employees," "weekly production payroll hours," "average hourly work week," "estimated lag time," and "invoice lag time."

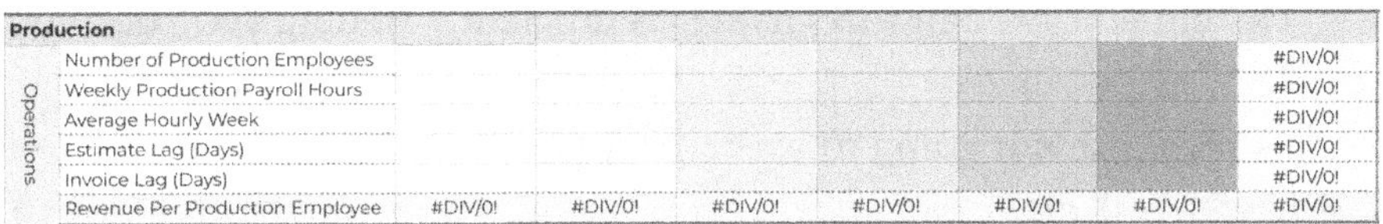

Number of Production Employees							#DIV/0!
Weekly Production Payroll Hours							#DIV/0!
Average Hourly Week							#DIV/0!
Estimate Lag (Days)							#DIV/0!
Invoice Lag (Days)							#DIV/0!
Revenue Per Production Employee	#DIV/0!	#DIV/0!	#DIV/0!	#DIV/0!	#DIV/0!	#DIV/0!	#DIV/0!

Your scorecard might look a lot different from this one. You certainly don't have to do it this way. Perhaps you don't even know what half of these calculations mean. That's okay. There are plenty of books out there that can help you understand them.

The point of this one right now is not to teach you how to calculate these metrics, but to make sure you choose some metrics to check in on every week. Remember the flight from NY to LA? Pilots are constantly

---

[27] Technically, you don't multiply by exactly 30, but you multiply by the quotient of 365/12, which is about 30.416

checking altitude, speed, and other things like that. Pick the metrics, the speed and altitude of your business, which affect your business and check in on them consistently so you can course correct before you end up in Canada. Even though it's a very beautiful place.

Pro Tip: You can copy our spreadsheet templates at

RestorationMillionaire.com/resources, so you don't have to build out all these calculations on your own.

Or, if you want a pro tip on steroids, you can use Albi—that's the restoration software company that I started, and my team built out an *insanely* user-friendly dashboard that's easy to understand, easier to use, and far more pleasant than any spreadsheets, even the ones I created. The math's the same, but the experience is much better with Albi.

The big takeaway in this chapter is efficiently finding your destiny, as quickly as possible.

As such, I'm not going to waste your time—we're almost done!

If you will *monitor your metrics* weekly, you're far more likely to hit your goal; by putting all four the of the major sections together, you'll have a snapshot of where you're at on your journey, increasing your chance of success and decreasing the chance you run into monumental problems.

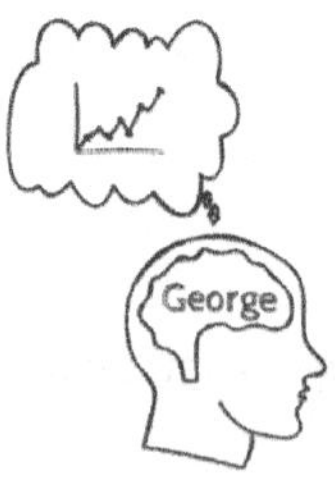

Georges, you probably already have some great metrics that you monitor. Make sure you include your team on this, too!

And Jack's, if the idea of looking at the numbers seems a little scary to you, just remember that you get to do it with your people. You've got this!

Now, of course, the other piece of this is ensuring you have the right people in place to execute on those metrics. Don't worry! That's what we're going to talk about next, in chapter eleven.

Momentum Trigger

For this chapter, your mission is pretty simple:

1) Go online to RestorationMillionaire.com/resources and download your own, free Restoration Scorecard™, if you don't already have another one that you look at on a regular basis. (If our scorecard seems too detailed or intimidating, or it's missing some critical details, it's very easy to edit.)

2) Pick a recurring weekly time to go over your Restoration Scorecard™ with your core leadership team. *Put that time on the calendar!*

Restorer's Recap

- When you correct your course frequently, on a plane or in your business, you will end up much closer to where you want to go. Can you imagine if a pilot only checked their heading every hour? They'd end up making huge, midway course corrections.
- In business, most restorers (and other small-business owners) only check the important metrics of their business, such as sales data, marketing analytics, and cashflow, once a quarter or even only once a year. By allowing such long gaps in-between checkups, problems are for more likely to happen. Instead, you should have a regular cadence of checking on the key data within your company.

CHAPTER 11:
The X Commandments of Hiring, Firing, & Inspiring

New Tools

In this chapter, we're going to discuss two useful tools!

The first is from Robert Glazer's book, *Elevate: Push Beyond Your Limits and Unlock Success in Yourself and Others* where he offers a simple illustration to describe the four types of performers at your company:

1. Unicorns (Star): These "unicorns" are the ones you hope to keep on as long as possible before they outgrow your company. At some point, they'll most likely move on to start their own.
2. A-players: You probably already know who these people are. Whether they've been promoted to manager already or are in your potential candidates, they see the direction of the company and are in it for the long-term.
3. Hard choices: The majority of your employees will fall into this category. Most employees are not 'A-player' employees, and that's great -- every business needs technicians who only want to be excellent technicians.
4. Underperformers: Self-explanatory; don't hold on to them longer than necessary.

The second tool we're going to discuss are my X Commandments for Hiring, Firing, & Inspiring:

I. Don't Hire Slow-Growers
II. Don't Fire Anyone. Transition Them
III. Don't Rely on "Vibe Checks"
IV. Don't Confuse Hustlers for Managers
V. Don't Promote Solely on Loyalty
VI. Do Use Golden Handcuffs
VII. Do Show Your Appreciation
VIII. Do Be Willing to Hire Specialists
IX. Do Remind Them of the 4D Dream™
X. Do Make 3 Key Hires

When you visit an Apple Store, you walk in, and not only is the place full of cool electronics, but each of the employees at the Genius Bar seems genuinely excited to be there. That's the kind of company I can get behind!

It's one thing to talk about how amazing Steve Jobs is as a leader, but what amazes me is that every Apple employee, all the way down to those on the frontline helping me fix my iPhone, seem to be innovative, "hip" people who are excited about their job. There's also a sort of cultural feeling that Apple gives off at every interaction the public has with their company... and I kind of dig it.

From the billboard to the employees, to the iPad, the whole company seems to be screaming: "We're creative, innovative, and hip!" And even though Steve Jobs has passed, the company appears to be pushing forward without him.

I guess Steve Jobs' famous dream of "putting a dent into the universe" will keep going on, even though he's no longer with us.

The Strong Company Culture

Remember back in chapter five, when I suggested that every restoration founder needs a 4D Dream™? Well, if you're going to make that huge, gigantic, amazing dream happen, you're going to need the right people to make it happen.

Finding and attracting the right people is difficult, but it's critical. You've got to be able to attract those who are going to propel your company forward, who are "drinking the same Kool-Aid," as everyone else, if you will.

What makes a company successful, is not just having a list of SOPs (although that's helpful). More importantly success doesn't even depend on having this one great leader. The founder of the Walt Disney Company passed away decades ago, and yet, the company is still known for its innovation in storytelling. Walt Disney, Apple, and others are successful today because of the cultures the companies have maintained.

Take a look at the effective, albeit controversial, work culture represented in Wolf of Wall Street. Most of us would agree that Jordan Belfort's work culture was toxic. But you couldn't say that the culture wasn't strong. In the same way that Apple's workplace culture has managed to seep into every area of their company, Belfort managed to accomplish the same in his company. And, on Wall Steet, it worked: Belfort established an environment that thrived on fast-paced decisions and a hustler mentality; he placed low value on honesty and high value on cash returns. As soon as everyone bought into his culture, each employee reaped the benefits (until they didn't of course).

Now, whether the culture is healthy is another debate entirely. But what made it powerful was Belfort's ability to hire people to fit and buy into that culture.

Whether you have an innovative culture, a hustler culture, a sales culture, a transparent culture... whatever your culture is, you need to be able to define that culture, then, go find and attract the people that you need to continue those values and perpetuate that culture.

We'll talk more in the next chapter about your mission, vision, and core values, but for now I want to help you with a simple task, one that's difficult—I want to help you know how to hire, fire, and inspire people.

Georges, building a company culture is something you've probably already excelled at, and I bet people love working for you. Great work!

At Albi, we've developed a very strong culture. We're a place of hustlers, of go-getters. It's a fast-paced environment where we've grown 300 percent, year-over-year, since we started, and we're just getting going. We're really, really into growth. And here's the interesting thing about growth—not everyone loves it.

We've managed to develop such a strong growth culture that new hires who don't enjoy that type of growth, will often walk themselves out the front door, with no hard feelings. I've had several conversations with people who, after a couple weeks, very kindly let me know that, "Alex, I see what y'all are doing here, and I respect it. The truth is, you all are running so fast, I can't keep up, and frankly, that's not me. I'm going to find something else."

Again, these are great people who've gone on to become amazing employees elsewhere, but they just don't quite fit the growth culture we've managed to develop here at Albi, and they don't want the pressure of having to be something they're not.

Picture it like drinking your favorite beverage—whether coffee, a Gatorade, tea, scotch, or a soda. Drinks taste the best when there's a singular, full-bodied, robust flavor. That's why most "single origin" coffees and wines cost more than blends, and why "single malt Scotch" is typically considered more valuable—when you pick up a drink, you don't want to taste a little soda, a little wine, a little milk. You want to have one smooth, bold flavor.

The benefit of this is, as you define your company culture, and work on keeping it the same, eventually, you'll attract the people who love that type of culture and they'll do their part to keep the culture "pure," if you will. For instance, recently, I had several team members come forward to let me know that a particular manager wasn't working the "Albi" way. No one was gossiping, nor were they even complaining, in the traditional sense. They just wanted me to be on the lookout for something that didn't mesh with our values. After investigation, it was easy to see that they were right—this particular manager was a great person, but they weren't working the way the rest of the company works.

That's the power of having a strong company culture—other employees that have bought into that culture, don't want to see it diluted. They'll stand up for the culture that they happily joined, and bring up inconsistencies when they spot them.

If you want to create that type of company culture, you've got to define what your culture is (or what you want it to be), then hire, fire, and inspire, accordingly.

That's the principle, and it's pretty simple: hire according to the culture you want, and fire (or transition), when someone's values aren't aligned. Then, as the leader, continually inspire others to live up to the company culture.

Over time, if you ensure that you hire and let go of employees based on the culture you're trying to build, you'll have enough momentum, that the other employees will help ensure the momentum continues—it's kind of like a Hula Hoop: while they're difficult to get spinning, once you do, you only have to give it a little push to keep it moving.

X Commandments of Hiring, Firing, & Inspiring

Now, "Hire, Fire, & Inspire," is an easy thing to say, but a harder thing to implement.

I've developed 10 Commandments of Hiring, Firing, & Inspiring that will help you keep that philosophy moving.

If you follow these, you'll be well on your way to creating a strong company culture that's aligned to the values that you want to keep.

I: Don't Hire Slow Growers

If you're following the Restoration Millionaire Method™, your company's not going to grow a little. It's going to grow massively, year, over year, over year. Not only that, but you as the leader will be forced to grow—in your leadership skills, in your patience and in your ability to handle stress. So, if you're reading this, whatever else is part of your company culture, I know growth is.

And here's what you don't want to do—you don't want to hire people that aren't growing enough to keep up with the pace of your company.

In his book *Elevate: Push Beyond Your Limits and Unlock Success in Yourself and Others,* Robert Glazer offers a simple example that describes the four types of performers at a growth-oriented company:

1. Unicorns (Star): These "unicorns" are the ones you hope to keep on as long as possible before they outgrow your company, because they are actually outpacing the growth of your company, pulling it with them. These are rare, but they're amazing to have on your team. They're like the Clydesdales that are pulling the entire Budweiser carriage forward.

2. A-players: You probably already know who these people are. Whether they've been promoted to manager already or are in your potential candidates, they see the direction of the company and are in it for the long-term. They are in lock-step with the growth of the company, learning and growing with it. Likely, your A-players find the work both challenging and exhilarating, and they're likely to want to stay on as long as possible.

3. Hard choices: Many of your employees will fall into this category—these are those who are certainly growing themselves; they're hard-workers who are often earning promotions and transforming their own capabilities. But, unfortunately, they just aren't' growing as fast as the rest of the company.

4. Underperformers: Those who are not growing much and are falling further and further behind the growth of the company, and they are, in some sense "easy" to let go of (Although it's never really easy to fire someone. More on that later).

According to Glazer, each team member has their own growth rate. Meanwhile, the company has its own growth rate. Optimally, everyone would be growing together, but in reality, some grow at the same pace as the company (or perhaps even faster), and most will grow slower, if you're at a high-growth company. According to Glazer, that means that the majority of your employees will probably be "hard choices," those that are not bad employees, but they're struggling to keep up with the pace you've set for your company.

So, Unicorns make the choice easy—- you keep them, as long as you can. A-Players are a perfect fit, challenged by the work you do, and happy to continue on as long as the company keeps moving forward. Hard-choices are just that—people that present difficult decisions to make, and again, you'll have a lot of these to make, typically.

Finally, Underperformers are also a fairly "easy" choice, even if that choice isn't easy to enact—you can probably think of an employee or two, right now, that you probably should have let go some time ago, but you just couldn't' face the music and fire them.

Well, that brings me to II—and my position is, you don't have to "fire" anyone.

II: Don't Fire Anyone. Transition Them

Firing an employee can feel a bit like breaking up with a girlfriend (or boyfriend). It's emotional for everyone involved, and it's a tough but necessary conversation that ultimately leads to growth through separation.

While I've fired a number of employees in the past, I've never once enjoyed it. But, I have learned a valuable lesson, particularly in the marketplace today (2023): I choose to view letting someone go as "transitioning" them from the company to a place where they are a better fit.

Again, I'm taking it for granted you didn't hire someone who's a jerk or who's stealing from your company. We're talking about decent people who just don't have the same personal values that your company does. No hard feelings—in those cases, it's best to let them go so that they're finding something better for themselves.

Unless they're flagrantly violating general morals and ethics, here's what we're talking about:

You've hired someone who checks all the boxes as far as typical employee qualities go (honest, hard-working, loyal). As the quarter progresses, his performance doesn't. He misses his goal on each business review, and though his attitude isn't necessarily negative, it doesn't contribute to the empowering culture you're trying so hard to cultivate. You can see the disappointment in himself every time he misses his goal–but do you keep him on while the rest of the team is smashing their numbers? While he may be an awesome person, he isn't able to buy into the culture that you've set.

Here's what I suggest in that scenario:

Gently confirm the employees' suspicions, that they aren't he right fit, here. Then, you can even give them a two-week notice so they have time to find another position that fits better for them. That gives the under-performer the choice to quit on the spot or use the two weeks to find another job that he'll be a better fit for.

In his book, Startup Santa: A Toymaker's Tale of 10 Business Lessons Learned from Timeless Toys, serial entrepreneur Brad Pedersen notes a conversation he had with Dave Liniger, the cofounder of RE/MAX. Liniger said that his biggest mistake in business was not firing fast enough. So, while it may be hard, you've simply got to let the underperformers go, and transition them into something else.

Transitioning those who don't fit serves two purposes:

1. It shows your current employees the level of effort and dedication it takes to do well in the standards you've set. They learn this environment is not for everyone, and that's OK.

2. It shows your employees (including those you've fired) you care about their well-being: Letting fear keep you from firing underperforming employees is not only hurting your business but holding back others on your team. Consider your staff, who often feels the impact of low performers even more than you do. Keeping employees like that could lead to further corruption of the healthy culture you're establishing.

As we mentioned in earlier chapters, be proactive not reactive with your teams. Check in with your managers and listen to their feedback. If they see there is room for improvement in one of their coworkers, you want them to feel comfortable coming to you about it.

III: Don't Rely on "Vibe Checks"

Have you ever hired someone simply because:

- They passed the vibe check
- They just really, really needed a job
- Their resume looked awesome (so you never even bothered to vet them)

Well, good news—if you said "yes" to any of the above, you're an entrepreneur. As we said earlier, we commonly come from chaotic backgrounds, and we often choose to see past somewhat obvious flaws.

When you first start hiring, you're often hiring your buddies, your next-door neighbor, and anyone you can get your hands on. When you're at a $1 million or less in revenue, and someone says, "I know someone who's looking for work..." you think "Thank God, what's their number?"

I get it – it's somewhat unavoidable, at first.

But eventually, you've got to move past that, and have a more well-thought-out process for hiring, with some sort of vetting process that's better than "I'd like to have a beer with them..."

If you simply hire those who pass your simple "vibe check," even if they do happen to be hard workers, you could end up with another problem: too many Jacks or Georges on your team, because, whatever you happen to be, you attracted and hired similar people.

So, you need to establish a hiring process, one that goes beyond "vibe checks" and "gut feelings."

One of the best ways to hire (and fire!) people, is by listing out your core values, then using those to be the judge – this removes a lot of the emotion from the process, and you. Most underperformers can even judge for themselves whether they fit the list of values, or not. (We'll go over more about your mission, vision, and values in the next chapter!)

IV: Don't Confuse Hustlers for Managers

Owners often confuse hustle for leadership skills. You may be tempted to use promotion as a reward for your unicorns and/or A-players, and sometimes, it can be. But typically, a promotion requires new expertise, and usually involves a new level of human interaction and people skills. Hustle and people skills are not the same thing.

You can have one, or both, or neither. If you have an A-player that you want to reward—and you should!—then consider whether or not a promotion is the best choice. If they have the skills (or can build them) for the new role, great. If not, consider a raise, more vacation time, or even company stock as alternatives.

V: Don't Promote Solely on Loyalty

Similar to hustle, many of us want to promote employees solely because of their loyalty. We'll overlook a lack of experience, a lack of skills, or lack of leadership potential and promote loyal employees just because they've been through it with us.

In the 1960s, Laurence J. Peter explained potential issues with this kind of thinking. According to "The Peter Principle," as long as employees continue to perform well, they often get promoted to the next highest position, despite not having any skills to support their transition. Their previous good work is used as justification to reward them. The better they continue to perform, the higher up the pyramid they climb. But at some point on the growth ladder, a promotion sets them up to fail, not succeed.

Of course, I often promote from within, but I don't rely solely on loyalty as the factor. Instead, I look at skills. If you're a salesperson who also has leadership potential, you're headed to manager. But without the critical leadership skills, I'd rather pay you more for your work, and let you continue in your current role, then promote you to a position that would frustrate you and everyone around you.

VI: Do Use Golden Handcuffs

Now, we come to our first "Do," after going over five "Don'ts"!

You want to incentivize those who are loyal to you and your company, especially those who support your vision. So, how do you figure out whether a loyal employee should handle more responsibility or if they should continue to excel as a technician? When faced with a similar situation, I've used "The Golden Handcuff Agreement."

Using Golden Handcuff agreements can be a great way to incentivize your best employees. If they aren't right for a promotion, but deserve a higher reward than standard compensation, use an agreement to demonstrate how much you appreciate their hard work. Common agreements include:

- Annual bonuses
- Student loan repayment benefits
- Company cars
- Relocation allowances
- 401k benefits

There are tons of options for Golden Handcuff agreements, but the goal isn't to find the shiniest toy and dangle it in front of your employee, nor is it to make them feel like they can't leave. Your goal is to communicate how much you value what they have to offer; in doing so, you create new excitement for their role.

Golden Handcuff agreements ensure your employees know exactly where they fit within your company, thus ultimately negating the "Peter Principle." I suggest offering these agreements only after clarifying that their lack of promotion is not a punishment, but the best possible fit for them.

VII: Do Show Your Appreciation

You must find ways to connect with your employees and provide fulfillment in their roles, while simultaneously inspiring loyalty to the company. Below are just a few real-life examples of how we gave back to our community at Romexterra and Albi:

- Helped pay for jerseys for both local basketball and soccer teams
- Held all-inclusive quarterly retreats
- Provided monthly gym memberships
- Hired a private chef to cook breakfast and lunch for team members

When you devote energy and resources into something that doesn't directly benefit your business, you show your employees what your company values.

VIII: Do Be Willing to Hire Specialists

Be willing to hire specialists, particularly as you grow.

In the early stages, you're probably looking for those who can do it all—people who are willing to try anything and have enough general skill to do a little sales, a little technical work, a little managing, a little invoicing. But the more you grow, the less efficient this type of work is. Instead, as your restoration company grows, you'll want to look for those with highly specialized skills, which means, often, you'll have to look outside the company, because, up to this point, you've hired generalists.

So, going back to Commandment IV: Don't Promote Only on Loyalty, be willing to look outside the company for those with special skills, to fill needed roles in management, sales, or technical roles.

IX: Do Remind Them of the 4D Dream™

When I walk into Albi offices, I can feel energy in the air. Each person is excited to tell me how they crushed their goal, improved their performance, or doubled their efforts against an obstacle. They're just as stoked about the trajectory of the company as I am. It isn't just their overly competitive nature; it's the desire of every single person trying to accomplish the same, clear, dream:

We've made our dream crystal clear to every employee who joins our staff: We're going to IPO.

When we do, many of our employees who own equity in the company will become millionaires. So, our people believe in the dream because we've made it crystal clear for them, and they know how it will affect them. I remind them, constantly, of where we're headed, and that they're going to be rewarded.

I rarely ask my employees to work after hours–they volunteer because of the value they place in the work they do. I don't have to ask for feedback on their peers' performance–they readily provide it if they see a problem. They are all in.

Don't all companies wish their team members cared enough about the trajectory of the business to hold their peers accountable? So how did I achieve the dream team? For us, it's about what we can do for them–not what they can do for us.

If you want to see your company grow, you must first pursue the growth of your team. Since the beginning, our dream at Albi was to build a company that would IPO within the next ten years, and we offer opportunities for Albi team members to purchase equity from the company, and actively track how the company is progressing. Not only does this build trust through transparency, but it incentivizes our employees to put in that much more effort.

X: Do Make 3 Key Hires

There are three key hires every fast-growing restoration company needs to make. You won't need all these on day one, but you will definitely need them if you want to become a world-class restoration company. I put this one last, because you'll need to implement the other IX Commandments here, meaning you can't just promote someone else based on loyalty or hustle. These are three key roles for which you'll want highly experienced professionals:

1. An Experienced Production Manager
Consider looking in HVAC, plumbing, or any other 24/7 service industry for previous experience.
2. An Experienced Sales Manager
Check out experience team leaders in the auto-body industry—they're already experts at dealing with insurance companies.
3. An Experienced Office Manager
Consider finding someone who's worked in other home-service-management companies.

For all three of these positions, you'll want someone who knows not only how to lead a team, but who can build a team.

For just a minute, consider some of the greatest brands in the world—NIKE, Apple, Disney, BMW, Ferrari, Coca-Cola, Microsoft... how many of those are still run by the original founders?

None, on my list—that's because the founders left behind a *legacy.* You want the same thing in your company: you want to leave a legacy so strong, that others carry it on, even when you aren't there—you want to make room for their dreams so that they find a home in yours.

If you can develop a company whose culture is strong, you can have a legacy that outpaces even your own life... if your dream's big enough, and your culture strong enough.

Go get that culture.

Momentum Trigger

This chapter's momentum trigger is going to use Robert Glazer's system of determining performance and a corresponding reward system.

Here's how to do the Momentum Trigger:

1) First, list each of your key employees (think sales manager, production manager, office manager, etc.).
2) Note whether each employee is:
    a. A Unicorn who's growing faster than your company
    b. An A-player who's growing as fast as your company
    c. A Hard choice who's growing, but growing slower than your company

    OR

    d. An Underperformer who's simply not growing
3) Decide this week what you're going to do for each employee in the above categories. If they're a unicorn or A-player, reward them somehow. If they're a hard-choice, decide how to get them to improve. If they're an underperformer consider transitioning them.

If you do the three steps above for your key employees, instantly, your company will be on a better path to creating the culture you need to execute on the future of your dreams.

Restorer's Recap

- X Commandments of Hiring, Firing, & Inspiring:
    I. Don't Hire Slow-Growers
    II. Don't Fire Anyone. Transition Them
    III. Don't Rely on "Vibe Checks"
    IV. Don't Confuse Hustlers for Managers
    V. Don't Promote Solely on Loyalty
    VI. Do Use Golden Handcuffs
    VII. Do Show Your Appreciation
    VIII. Do Be Willing to Hire Specialists
    IX. Do Remind Them of the 4D Dream™
    X. Do Make 3 Key Hires
- Strong company culture positions a company for growth.
- Don't think so much of "bad" or "good" company culture. Instead, think "strong" company culture. Your goal should be to create a pure company culture that is seen, heard, and felt by your employees, your subcontractors, and your customers.
- There are four types of performers in every company:
- Unicorns (Star): These "unicorns" are the ones you hope to keep on as long as possible before they outgrow your company. At some point, they'll most likely move on to start their own.
- A-players: You probably already know who these people are. Whether they've been promoted to manager already or are in your potential candidates, they see the direction of the company and are in it for the long-term.

- Hard choices: The majority of your employees will fall into this category. Most employees are not 'A-player' employees, and that's great -- every business needs technicians who only want to be excellent technicians.
- Underperformers: Self-explanatory; don't hold on to them longer than necessary

$5 MILLION+: REPLICATE & SCALE

CHAPTER 12: Get Your Head in the Clouds

How To Set Your Mission, Vision, & Core Values

"94 percent of problems in business are systems driven and only 6 percent are people driven."
—W. Edwards Deming

New Tool

In this chapter, we're going to talk about defining your company's mission, vision, and values. We'll spend the most time on mission.

To find and define your company's "mission," use WALT:

> ***W**rite down each of your company's offerings.* ("We reconstruct homes destroyed by fires." "We clean up water damage.")
>
> ***A**sk why?* For each offering, ask "Why?" Then, keep asking why. A good rule of thumb is to ask three to five times until you have a concrete reason for why your company performs each task.
>
> ***L**ook for trends in your whys.* What answers come up frequently for each offering?
>
> ***T**ype it all up.* Put the final product into a nice, written document. Wordsmith it. That's now your company's mission.

A lot of companies talk about mission, vision, and values, and some of them can be quite inspirational. Check out this mission statement, by JetBlue:

"To inspire humanity—both in the air and on the ground."[28]

Or this one, from LinkedIn:

"To connect the world's professionals to make them more productive and successful."[29]

Or this one from Amazon:

"To be Earth's most customer-centric company, where customers can find and discover anything they might want to buy online, and endeavors to offer its customers the lowest possible prices."[30]

Don't you just feel ready to *do* something with these sorts of statements? I sure do. And you know what? Employees probably do, too.

Employees want nothing more than to show up to work and feel like they're part of something. And that's what we're going to talk about in this chapter—how to set the thermostat for the whole gang, the whole company, to inspire them toward a future.

Now, if that sounds like a little bit of a repeat of chapter five, don't worry—I'm not going to waste your time. In chapter five, we discussed your 4D Dream™ for you. In this very short chapter, we're going to go over a simple tool to take your dreams and formalize them in three ways: a mission statement, a company vision, and your company values.

---

[28] "JetBlue Mission Statement 2023: JetBlue Mission & Vision Analysis." Biggest Mission Statements Collection - Mission Statement Academy, January 27, 2021. https://mission-statement.com/jetblue/.

[29] "LinkedIn Professional Community Policies." LinkedIn. Accessed November 28, 2023. https://www.linkedin.com/legal/professional-community-policies.

[30] Cuofano, Gennaro. "Amazon Mission Statement and Vision Statement in a Nutshell." The Four Week MBA, October 1, 2023

Mission, Vision, Values

Companies use their mission, vision, and values as three components that set the tone for the entire enterprise. They tell the world what they're all about, what they're going to do, and how they're going to get there.

In truth making, vision, and values are all a little bit related, but slightly different. Most large companies have all three, some have only two or one, but almost everyone agrees that they're all important.

In this chapter, we're going to talk about all three, and I'll give you the tools to develop all of them, quickly.

Now, I could tell you why they're so important, or I could *show* you why they're so important, by sharing with you one of my *favorite* mission statements out there. Here it is:

> *The mission of The Walt Disney Company is to entertain, inform and inspire people around the globe through the power of unparalleled storytelling, reflecting the iconic brands, creative minds and innovative technologies that make ours the world's premier entertainment company.*[31]

Dang.

Now *that's* a mission statement.

Can you imagine working there, and being inspired to be "unparalleled" at "storytelling" to reflect "Iconic" characters at a "creative" and "innovative" company?

Now, this isn't just all fluff. Since the company's founding, the man Walt Disney himself won twenty-six Oscars [32]—no one else has come

---

[31] "Disney - Leadership, History, Corporate Social Responsibility." The Walt Disney Company, March 2, 2020. https://thewaltdisneycompany.com/about/.

[32] Grein, Paul. "Walt Disney Still Holds These 5 Oscar Records, Nearly 60 Years after His Death." Billboard, May 25, 2023

even close. But since the man Walt passed away, his company has gone on to win over 100 more![33]

What Walt did on his own has paled in comparison to what he's left behind, and what others have done by building on what he started and creating an even better future.

So, how can *we* create a mission statement, a vision statement, or a list of company values that has some sort of inspiration like that? I mean, is that even possible in restoration?

I think so.

A Culture of Dreamers

At Albi, a unique, dual-sided culture exists: either our newest hires are walking themselves out the door, or they are working their tooshies off. As I tell my team in our performance meetings, this is the NFL, not your local high school's football team. But that's not meant to intimidate; instead of being overwhelmed, my team is excited; rather than scared, they're emboldened. When it's time to leave, they choose to stay – not because anyone is forcing them, or simply because they'll get paid overtime, but because they take pride in their work. They know what they do each day matters. Each person at Albi *wants* to be at Albi, and nowhere else. Why? Because we have some audacious goals, and they all *know* it.

A dreamer culture, though it sounds like something you'd find at The Walt Disney Company, is an essential piece to the restoration millionaire puzzle. If your dream is to impact you and your team's lives forever, you need to make sure your employees experience three things: fulfillment, motivation, and commitment.

---

[33] Murray, Emily. "Disney's History with the Academy Awards." DVC Shop, March 27, 2022. https://dvcshop.com/disneys-history-with-the-academy-awards/.

Finding Fulfillment

What makes you get out of bed in the morning? For you as an entrepreneur, it might be your instinct to work hard no matter what's put in front of you, or maybe it's your need to do right by those working under you. Whatever it is, there's a reason you're the bootstrapper, not your team. So, what about your employees?

Find employees who believe in your vision *and* are fulfilled by their role in achieving it; they'll bring you that much closer to that dream.

Magnifying Motivation

Fulfillment is one part of the equation for good performance; the other part is motivation. When I walk into Albi offices, I can feel excitement in the air. Each person is excited to tell me how they crushed their goal, improved in their performance, or doubled their efforts against an obstacle. They're just as stoked about the trajectory of the company as I am. It isn't just their overly competitive nature; it's the desire of every single person trying to accomplish the same dream. Every person aboard the Albi ship knows its destination and is hard-wired to do everything they can to get it there quickly and successfully. And while money isn't the only incentive, it's still one heck of a motivator.

When your employees sit down for a quarterly review, naturally you discuss their performance within the company. But when's the last time you had a mission statement to point to? When's the last time you had a huge vision that you could say, "Here's how you're helping us accomplish our goals!

Cementing Commitment

Finally, as a result of feeling fulfilled and motivated, your employees will become truly committed. Commitment toward the mission, vision, and values is essential—as I mentioned earlier, you won't get to where you want to go without them, so they better be in it for the long-game.

Mission, Vision, Values

If you can create solid mission, vision, and values for your entire company, you can achieve all of this, and more.

Just like we discussed in chapter five about the 4D Dream™, your mission, vision, and values must be clear and concise—everyone in your company should know exactly what you're aiming for, why you're asking for it, and how you're going to get there.

Alright, enough talk... I hope I've convinced you that you need a mission, vision, and values statement. Now, *how do you make them?*

Well, it's actually pretty easy:

Vision = Take it From Your 4D Dream™

If you recall from chapter five, we discussed the importance of having an audacious, detailed future vision, which we called your 4D Dream™. Without one, not only will you lose sight of the goal, but so will those around you. A giant dream gives you the motivation in the present to reach future goals. So, the good news, you already have a head start on this one—we're simply suggesting you take the parts of your 4D Dream™ and turn it into a crisp statement for your company.

So, revisit your 4D Dream™, and take the elements that have specifically to do with your current company. Then, create a nice, sweet, punchy statement. If you need a couple examples, here's a couple vision statements:

- Patagonia: "To save our home planet."
- LinkedIn: "Create economic opportunity for every member of the global workforce."

You'll probably notice how short these are! By starting with your 4D Dream™, you should be able to extract what's most important, and has to do *with your company.*

Values = Discover, Don't Create

Your company values are also fairly simple to find, and you probably already started thinking about them in the last chapter, eleven, when we discussed the X Commandments of Hiring, Firing, & Inspiring.

Your company values are not wish lists that you *wished* your company cared about. They are the true characteristics that matter most to the key stakeholders. Namely, the founders.

After growing at a break-neck speed, my father and I brought in a consultant to help us organize Romexterra. We had several million in revenue, which was a blessing, but we were struggling with the big-picture strategy on what to do next. Thankfully, our consultant asked us some simple questions, one of which was:

"What do you and your father *both* value?"

That sounds like a pretty simple question, and maybe it should be. But it turns out, most of us entrepreneurs have been running *so quickly* that we haven't stopped to really think about what we value in life.

So, when the consultant asked my father and me this question, we didn't know the answer. We locked ourselves in a room for an hour and asked each other: "What do *you* value?"

As we started discussing, our first answers were wildly different. I valued more money; my father valued more security. I valued getting the job done right, my father valued getting it done on time. I valued giving our employees the opportunity to make more money based on performance, my father valued steady paychecks.

Around we went, for hours. Importantly, we weren't trying to *judge* what our values were. We were trying to be honest, because that's what the consultant said to do. This wasn't about fabricating some fluffy words that could go on social media. We were honestly trying to ask ourselves *What do I care about?"*

Five hours later, and my father and I did have a short list of ideals we both cared tremendously about. These may sound overly simplistic to you, but here it goes:

- Honesty
- Transparency
- Doing the right thing

See? Notice how we didn't say "world peace," as if we were trying to become Miss America. Also, we didn't try to make our company values sound hipper than they really are.

You may not have a partner or cofounder, but it doesn't matter. The process of finding your company values is pretty much the same: You just ask yourself what you care about. These values become exactly what you use to train your employees, transition them, and promote them. If someone doesn't share *any* of your company's values... I wouldn't even hire them, no matter how good of a worker they are.

Mission = The Big One

When you're defining your company's vision, you can simply refer to your own 4D Dream™ and take the parts that have to do with this company. When you're looking for your company values, you aren't trying to change anything, you're simply asking, *What do we care about?*

But your mission is going to take more work for you. For starters, let's talk about what a company mission is. And, in fact, instead of talking about it, let's show a few.

Chipotle has a very simple one, to provide "Food with integrity."

Starbucks made theirs very poetic:

With every cup,
with every conversation,
with every community—
we nurture the limitless possibilities
of human connection.

At Albi, we didn't get near that fancy with our mission statement, which is:

"To propel restoration forward."

What's *your* mission statement? Remember, this is where you tell the world, "Hey, this is what we're all about." And defining yours doesn't have to be difficult or fancy (although, I do kind of dig how Starbucks put theirs into a small poem!).

Make It Clear

I get that your thinking *What's the difference between my vision statement and my mission statement?*

Truthfully, while I think they're both important, if you only have one or the other, that's fine. But regardless, make it *clear* for everyone on your team. When I say clear, I like to think of *Mission: Impossible.*

Have you ever watched a *Mission: Impossible* movie? I love me some Tom Cruise. And typically, toward the beginning of the film, someone sends Ethan Hunt, Tom Cruise's character, a fancy gizmo with the famous lines, "Your mission, should you choose to accept it..." Whatever comes after that simple intro is the crux upon which the whole movie will hinge—how will Hunt need to save the world *this* time?

That line "Your mission..." is a clever device the scriptwriters use to center the entire audience around a common goal—it gets all of us watching the film pumped up and cheering for Hunt as he faces trial after trial, evil soldiers, impossible villains, and difficult circumstances. By painting the picture of the mission very clearly (and usually making it sound dire!) the filmmakers are able to quickly rally the audience onto Hunt's side and cheer for him to the end.

Similarly, your vision, mission, and values statements need to be able to rally the troops. They need to be clear and concise. They must be repeated frequently enough that everyone knows exactly what you're talking about.

Again, if you only do one or two of the three (mission, vision, and values), that's fine—just whatever you do, make what you choose to do, very clear. If you're able to do all that, and if every person in your company is bought into the plan with some real emotion, then there's almost nothing you can't face—in the same way that the 4D Dream™ will inspire you to push past difficulties, your statements can be the keys that unlock motivation for your employees.

So, you ready? Let's find your mission.

Develop Your Mission With WALT

And now we're at the crux of this chapter—how to find your company's *mission.*

Since I think The Walt Disney Company has done more to inspire their employees than just about any other company out there, I've taken the liberty of calling this "WALT," which stands for Write, Ask, Look, Type:

> ***W****rite down each offering your company provides.*
> ***A****sk "Why do we do this?" for each offering.*
> ***L****ook for trends in your whys.*
> ***T****ype up the top trends into a written document. This is your company's mission.*

W: Write

First, you need to *write down* every single thing your company does: "We reconstruct homes destroyed by fires." "We clean up water damage."

From there, you can get a little more descriptive, adding in meaningful words. "We *masterfully* reconstruct *beautiful* homes destroyed by fires." "We *quickly* clean up *all* water damage."

I find it's actually *also* helpful to add to the list anything your company does *differently* than the industry. For instance, "We take three steps back when we knock on a homeowner's door."

For Starbucks, if they were going through this exercise – and I imagine they did some version of it!—they may list off "Serve world-class beverages," or "Keep an impeccably clean front-of-house."

So, list off all your offers, being sure to fill in what you do differently and any specific descriptors, if you want.

A: Ask "Why?"

Now, for each of those items, ask, "Why do we do this?"

Why do you reconstruct beautiful homes? Why do you take three steps back from the door? Why do you handle every invoice within forty-eight hours?

Importantly, don't stop asking "Why?" after one answer. Some say that if you want the real answer to someone, you have asked "Why?" five, seven, or even *more* times to get the real truth. Let's say you wrote down the following:

"We clean up water damage."

Your first "Why?" may be, "Because we're good at it." Then, if you ask, "Why are we good at it?" you may put something like, "Because we care about quality." Then, if you ask again, you may realize the answer is, "We care about quality because *we're committed to world-class performance.*"

Now, imagine how "We're committed to world-class performance" sets the stage for a kick-ass mission statement!

You may have to ask yourself "Why?" five or more times, but don't stop until you get to the root reason for each line-item you listed in W: Write.

L: Look for Trends

Now, after you've drilled down to the basic whys, look at your list, and look for trends.

More likely than not, if you've really done a good job of trying to find the why behind what you do and the way that you do it, you'll notice something... certain words, concepts, and underlying reasons pop up, frequently. In fact, you may have the same why for almost *every single* line-item you originally wrote down.

Those are the whys that I'm' talking about. The ones that pop up time and time again in your reasons for doing what you do.

T: Type It Up

That's it—those common whys that stretched from offering to offering are your mission. You'll need to clean it up a little and check for grammar and punctuation, but honestly, you aren't looking for a Hallmark card or pageant speech; you want an authentic mission that is *clear* and *concise.*

Here's a quick example; to save time and space, I've only listed two offerings:

W: Write	We restore water-damaged homes.	We offer board-ups.
A: Ask "Why"?	Because we make money.	Because this would allow us to connect with the firefighters in the area
	We make money because we're good at what we do, and the community trusts us.	We want to connect with firefighters because we want them to trust us.
	We're good at what we do because quality is important to us.	
	We care about this community because we live here.	
L: Look for trends	"Community" "care" and "trust."	
T: Type It Up	Our mission is to be a company that our community trusts to restore their homes with quality and care.	

Boom!

See how when it's time to "type it up" the mission statement almost writes itself?

The Other Disney

After Walt Disney passed away, the company ran well for some time under his brother, Roy's leadership. But then, Roy passed away, also.

But, after going through a few other leaders, Roy E. Disney, Walt's nephew, came back to the company. He reminded the leadership of the company's core values and their roots, and asked if he could lead the animation studio, and they agreed. After he took it over, Roy E. Disney re-organized personnel and galvanized new creativity, and a new era of animation flourished, known today as Disney Renaissance. The new animation studio churned out hit after hit, starting with The Little Mermaid, then continuing with such blockbuster hits as Beauty and the Beast, the first animated film to be nominated for the Best Picture Oscar. Then came Aladdin, The Lion King (which grossed over $1 billion), Pocahontas, Mulan, and Tarzan.

How did Roy E. Disney do it? He had the same culture, the same "stuff" as his uncle and his father. He had a mission, and he knew exactly what it was.

Go get yours.

Momentum Trigger

Your Momentum Trigger for this chapter is get your mission statement completed.

Heres' what you do: Use WALT to figure it out. You may need to give yourself a couple one-hour sessions all by yourself so you can really think and dive into this. So, go onto your calendar, and block out the time you need. Then, use WALT to create a mission statement:

> ***W****rite down each offering your company provides.*
>
> ***A****sk "Why do we do this?" for each offering and keep asking why.*
>
> ***L****ook for trends in your whys.*
>
> ***T****ype up the top trends into a written document. This is your company's mission.*

Restorer's Recap

- Your "vision" is simply the 4D Dream™ we discussed in chapter five.
- Your "values" are fairly easy to define; What matters to you (and your cofounders)? What is most important? By these values, you should hire, fire, & inspire, as we discussed in chapter eleven.
- **To find your "mission," follow WALT:**

1) ***W****rite down each thing your company does.* ("We reconstruct homes destroyed by fires." "We clean up water damage.")

2) ***A****sk why?* For each thing your company does, drill down and ask "Why?" then keep asking why. A good rule of thumb is to ask three to five times until you have a very concrete reason for why you perform each of the tasks in step one.

3) ***L****ook for trends in your why.* What answers come up frequently?

4) ***T****ype it all up!* in a nice, written document. That's now your company's mission.

CHAPTER 13:
Use CREDIT to Build a Cash Cushion

"You do not rise to the level of your goals; you fall to the level of your systems."
—James Clear in Atomic Habits

New Tool

In this chapter, we're going to discuss how to build a three- to six- month cash cushion, using a simple method:

C-Credit line

R-Relationships

E-Extend payment terms

D-Deposits

I-Interest-free credit cards

T-Tie commissions to payments

Think of how you'd feel if you suddenly had a three to six-month window of cash available? What decisions would you be able to make? What bigger jobs would you say "yes" to? What better hires would you make? How much less stress would you feel?

Six months of extra cash in the bank can be a game-changer for your business, because you'll make vastly different decisions. You won't be bound by the constant "what if?" questions. You won't be thinking,

What if we have one bad month? What if that one big customer doesn't pay us on time? What if one of my key employees gets sick?

If you can develop a three to six-month cash supply, where all your bills would be paid, *even if* everyone stopped paying you, I can guarantee, your decisions are going to get a lot better, very quickly. You'll *only* be focused on growth, on making the best long-term decisions, not on making ones that only take care of today.

And that's what we're going to discuss in this chapter—how to create a cash cushion that gives you some breathing room. By the end, you'll have every tool you need to create a cash cushion that enables you to make the best decision in your business.

In restoration, while it's a high-profit-margin industry, you're constantly battling a cashflow problem: insurance companies pay you in thirty, sixty, or even ninety days, and yet, you often have to buy tools, rent equipment, fuel your trucks, and pay your subcontractors and employees well before that. Which means, there's always a gap between when you get paid, and when you have to pay out to do that same work. This gap becomes one of the biggest problems for most restorers—while they can land big jobs in this industry, fairly easily, they often end up with huge gaps that can eat them alive! That's why in one of the first chapters of this book we go over the 48-Hour Rule™, which helps you *shorten* the time that it takes for money to come *in.*

Now, in this chapter, we're going to go over how to *lengthen* the time that you have to *pay out.*

CREDIT

Remember back in chapter four, when we discussed what it feels like when there's less and less money in your bank account? Most business owners, when we see the bank account getting low, have a gut reaction that screams, *Cut costs; cut costs!*

Similarly, there's a normal feeling that occurs when your engine stalls as you're about to land. Without training, you'd follow your instinctual thoughts, which are, *Pull up! Pull up!*

But the reality is, in both instances, when you're approaching altitude-zero in your bank account, or when you're approaching altitude-zero because of a stall during a plane landing, what you need to do is *add power.* Specifically, in chapter four, we discussed the 48-Hour Rule™, which means, basically, to follow-up with every interested party every forty-eight business hours, until an invoice is paid.

I like to think of the 48-Hour Rule™ as "part one" to the cashflow discussion, and then what we're going to discuss is "part two," of that same talk. The 48-Hour Rule™ helps you collect cash as quickly as possible, what I'm about to explain will help you build a cash cushion *without* actually having to increase sales. Importantly, this chapter comes after the 48-Hour Rule™, because it's not a supplement to actually collecting cash that's owed to you. Truthfully, *nothing* is. You want to collect all money owed to you as quickly as possible. Period. Every time. If you only learn one thing, learn that.

But there are a few other tips and tricks to help you achieve that six-month cash cushion that is so elusive to most restorers. Here are the elements you have to create a cash cushion:

C-Credit line
R-Relationships
E-Extend payment terms
D-Deposits
I-Interest-free credit
T-Tie commissions to cashflow

Let's dive into each element by itself and explain how the entire model works together:

C-Credit Line

First and foremost, you can get a credit line. Now, again, you don't want to *over* utilize these. But, when used correctly, these can provide a huge lifeline to any business owners.

I told you a little of the story about the huge job that Romexterra landed because of our contact who worked with a Chicagoland Housing Authority complex. We won an eight-story water mitigation job that was a bit out of our league, but, thankfully, my buddy had all the right equipment to handle this job, and he pulled up, made us look like rockstars, and gave me pretty favorable terms to pay him back for subcontracting the work to him.

But here's the part I didn't tell you—we didn't get paid for years.

A huge, corporate competitor didn't like the fact that a smaller hotshot company took what would usually have been a nearly million-dollar job from them. So, they reported us as having charged far outside the normal bounds (which was totally silly – but like I said, they were mad at us).

The case, which ended up getting settled for a favorable amount for us a couple years later, got tied for several years after the work was completed. In the meantime, I had to pay my buddy and his team, our employees, equipment rentals, and other subcontractors. In total, the job *cost* us several hundred thousand dollars, and we didn't get paid on it for over two years after we'd paid all that out.

So, how did we survive in the meantime? Our line of credit.

We'd built up a good relationship with our local bank, and they'd given us a nice line of credit. A line of credit can be a lifesaver—if we *hadn't* had that, that job could have been our downfall. Which means we would have had to decide between risking taking it, and a hiccup, like the one that occurred, bringing us down, OR we would have had to pass on it altogether. Thankfully, we didn't have to make that choice. We were able to lean into the growth of our company and take a huge project, which brought us, eventually, tons of cash, and put a huge project and client on our company resume.

That's what building a cash cushion is all about—having the available funds, when you need them, to make the best decision for the longevity of your business. In our case, we may not even exist had we not had that line of credit.

R-Relationships

Relationships are key when you're trying to build up a cash cushion—just as I explained before, Our relationship with the bank is what allowed us to draw upon a credit line. Further, I had a relationship with my colleague who owned the other restoration company. While we ended up having to pay him before we got paid, he didn't make us pay him upfront, and, if we hadn't had those relationships, he would have been well within his rights to ask us to pay him before the work commenced.

There are two other relationships that matter, big time, when it comes to creating a cash cushion:

Supplier and subcontractor. I'll go more into detail with both of these later, but the key thing is: the better your relationships, the better your terms will be for payments.

E-Extend payment terms

With good relationships, you can ask for extended payment terms from a variety of sources. Again, two key ones are suppliers and subcontractors.

You ever heard the terms "net-60" or "net-30"? These terms may sound foreign, but they can be your friend when it comes to creating a cash cushion.

Here's how you use them:

You go ask your suppliers, particularly the larger ones, if you can pay them using net-30 or net-60 terms. Often, suppliers you've been ordering a ton from, such as Home Depot, Lowe's, or other corporate giants, will rather easily give you favorable payment terms. Which means, you can rent equipment, buy tools, etc., all on credit that allows you to pay them back over thirty, sixty, or even ninety days.

If you manage to get net-30 or net-60 terms with some of your largest suppliers, you'll be able to take on more work, and move out your payment window until *after* you're getting paid from many of your jobs. (This is assuming you're utilizing the 48-Hour Rule™ very, very well!).

Typically, with a large enough supplier, these sorts of terms are pretty easy to get (particularly if they know you order thousands of dollars' worth of equipment and materials from them).

The other group you can ask for extending payment terms are your subcontractors. Now, the trick is here, obviously, you need to do it in a way that they perceive as fair and equitable. The goal is to close the window between the time *you* get paid and when you're having to *pay out.* Subcontractors likely won't be able to wait as long as you do, but the longer you can get to wait, the better off you'll be, and if you create a fairly consistent timeframe that is predictable and reasonable, most subcontractors will agree to it.

D-Deposits

Upfront deposits can be a *life saver.* While most homeowners want to use their insurance to pay the totality of the bill, some jobs won't be covered by insurance, and/or the homeowner would rather just deal with themselves. In these cases, you can ask for a small amount, say 10 to 25 percent of the estimate to be paid up front.

The trick here is that you watch your *accounts receivable* so that you don't get upside-down on your work. In other words, if you're taking large amounts of deposits up front, it's very, very easy to misunderstand what's coming in and what's going out. I could share with you tons of stories of tradespeople who took large deposits up front, but then, weren't able to actually do the work because they messed up their own books; that's not a fun place to be!

I-Interest-free credit cards

Credit cards have an interesting billing method—first, credit cards have statement "closing date," which typically occurs monthly. That closing date will collect all the charges since the previous closing date and add them up onto a *statement.* Then, that statement goes out to you, and you have about thirty days to pay it, depending on your card terms.

That means, you have from the time you purchased something, until the end of your statement closing date, *plus,* you also have until that statement is *due.* Meaning, potentially, depending on when you used your credit card and when the statements go out, you have sixty days from the day you purchased something until that charge accrued any interest.

As an example, let's say that your statement's *closing* date is July 30th, and then that statement's *due* date is on August 30th. If you buy something on July *5th,* that charge will go on the July 30th *statement,* which will not be due until August 30th; so, you'd have a total of fifty days to pay it off before it collected interest!

Credit cards are pretty confusing, but the math works like this:

Days from purchase until next *statement closing date* + days until that statement's *due date* = Days until you need to pay it.

So, again, here's a scenario:

Let's say that you purchase something on January 12th, and the next statement closing date is January 20th, and the statement's due date is February 19th. In that case, you'd have a total of thirty-eight days to pay it off before interest accrued.

Here's how it looks:

Purchase date:	Janury12th
Next statement *closing* date:	January 20th
Next statement *due* date:	February 19th
Which would mean:	
From purchase date to statement closing date:	8 days
From closing date to due date:	30 days
Total days to pay:	38 days

While credit card companies seem to enjoy making this as confusing as possible, if you find your *statement closing date* and your *statement due date,* then, you can proactively plan how to use credit cards to your advantage, all without even paying interest.

T-Tie commissions to payments

I'm a huge believer in giving everyone a slice of the pie, particularly in restoration. You can pay nearly everyone on commission—from the crew chief to the production manager to the salesperson.

The trick is to simply ensure that you *tie commission to payments.* So, let's say that you pay a 10-percent sales commission on a job that's worth $10,000. In that case, you only give out that 10 percent commission when *you* get paid for the job. This does two things:

1) By tying commissions to payments, you'll ensure that you're never "upside-down" with commission checks—you'll only pay out, as money comes in.

2) This will incentivize your entire team to bill quickly and accurately. Everyone on your team will follow the 48-Hour Rule™, if for no other reason than, when you get paid, they get paid! Magically, they start caring a lot more about getting those invoices in on time!

The Quick & Dirty on "Accrual Accounting"

If you take the CREDIT system and apply it to your business, you'll easily build up a nice cash cushion, without having to do almost anything different. Let's say you pay your biggest vendors and suppliers on net-30 terms, you start paying your subcontractors every other Friday, and you use credit cards wisely. Then, on top of all that, you get a $100,000 credit line with the local bank.

Now, you'll have a nice cash cushion that will ease the pain between when you have to pay *out* for a job to your subs, employees, and vendors, and when you get money *in* from a job.

There is a trick, though, that you need to be aware of—with "net-30" due dates, credit card utilization, and invoices waiting to be paid, your accounting books are going to look a little confusing. The truth is, they *probably already do,* because you're almost never, ever paid the moment you finish work, so, you're always in this awkward waiting period, waiting for your accounting books to balance out. The moment you step into extending payment terms and the like, the books may even look a little more awkward, a bit like a Picasso painting where all the accounting is there, but it's a bit sideways.

So, to simplify matters and help you stay on track with where your cashflow really is, you'll want to ask your accountant to give you the numbers as if you were using *accrual accounting.*

Most likely, you're currently using *cash accounting,* which is a highly accurate picture of what really happened. So, cash accounting just says, "What money literally changed hands?" Cash accounting doesn't even get into who owes what or when, it just shows that, "Alex Duta started the month with $10,000, then $5,000 of expenses left his account, and a $7,000 deposit from an insurance company hit his account. So, he's ending this month with $12,000." That's cash accounting.

Accrual accounting isn't trying to answer the question for what money changed hands. Accrual accounting is saying, "Here's what work was 'accrued' or performed this month *even if,* it hasn't been paid yet." So, in other words, accrual accounting, is *not* just going to show you the amount of money that hit your bank. Rather, it's going to show you how much work you *performed,* as if you got paid. Accrual accounting will also show you what you *owe,* even if you didn't actually pay it quite yet. So, Let's say that in January you did $150,000 worth of work and you owe $100,000 for everything that you did that month—rent, employees, subcontractors, etc. Accrual accounting would say you "made" $50,000 that month, even though, likely, you didn't actually get any money or pay any money yet. Again, accrual accounting just means, "Here's what happened this time period, even if the money hasn't changed hands yet."

So, cash accounting:

"I don't know how much work we did or what we owe, but here's what literally happened to the cash."

Accrual Accounting:

"I don't know what happened to the cash, but I know who owes what."

Cash accounting is typically much more advantageous for tax purposes, so, you'll want your accountant to keep using that method to pay your taxes, but *you'll* want to also know the accrual accounting numbers, so that way you can figure out if you're doing more work or less work each month, and if you're owing more or less each month.

Georges! I don't think Jacks honestly care, but here's some info for you if you shift to accrual accounting and you see some new terms:

"Accounts receivable," simple means what others ow you.

"Accounts payable," simple means *what you owe.*

Don't Forget the 48-Hour Rule™

The CREDIT System is a very powerful method of ensuring you develop a cash cushion between when you get paid and when you have to pay out. But here's the deal—it only works if you're actually planning on bringing the money *in.*

In other words, if you aren't making sales or you aren't collecting invoices, the CREDIT system is just a patch, and, without the eventual cash coming in, it will fail.

So, above all, remember the 48-Hour Rule™. If you use that rule effectively, you'll be ensuring you get paid every thirty days, almost every time. Then, you can couple that with the CREDIT system, and the result will be that you have a nice amount of cash that allows you to make good, long-term decisions, not emergency decisions that stress you and your team out.

Momentum Trigger

You want to develop a cash cushion *before* you need it. If you wait until the last minute, you may have to say no to a big job or an opportunity that you could have otherwise said "yes" to.

The CREDIT system hits every area of your cash gap, so you can use it on an ongoing basis to check for ways to help develop that cash cushion. But I've created a prioritized checklist that will allow you to get started, *today* on creating that cash cushion. Importantly, this list is in order. You can go through it now, and as soon as you answer "no," to a question, then that can be your action-step for this chapter. So, let's say you answer "yes" to the first two questions, but no to the third, then the third question is where you need to focus, ASAP:

1) **Are all your commissions tied to payments?** If not, then stop here and put in a system to ensure that all commissions are paid as payments come in.

2) **Do you have a sizeable line of credit?** If not, then stop here and open a line of credit. Hint: start with banks you have an existing relationship with.

3) **Are all your big corporate vendors on net-30 or net-60 payment terms?** If not, then stop here and put your largest corporate vendors (think *Home Depot* or *Lowe's*) and ask them for extended payment terms.

4) **Do you have a *business* credit card that you can use to make big purchases?** If not, then stop here and open a business credit card.

Restorer's Recap

- The restoration industry enjoys excellent profit margins. Unfortunately, though, there's typically a large gap between when money goes *out* to subcontractors, employees, and vendors, and when money comes *in* from insurance companies. To erase this gap, restorers can first utilize the 48-Hour Rule™ to get invoices paid ASAP. Then, restorers can use the CREDIT system to extend when they have to pay.
- The CREDIT system of creating a cash cushion:
    - **C**-Credit line
    - **R**-Relationships
    - **E**-Extend payment terms
    - **D**-Deposits
    - **I**-Interest-free credit cards
    - **T**-Tie commissions to payments
- As a restoration company grows, you will have more money waiting to come in and bills waiting to be paid. Eventually, you'll want to ask your accountant to show you your books as per *accrual accounting.* Your accountant may suggest that, for tax purposes, you still utilize cash accounting.

CHAPTER 14:
The 4 Power Tools of Business

New Tool

In restoration, and in most businesses, there are four ways to solve every problem:

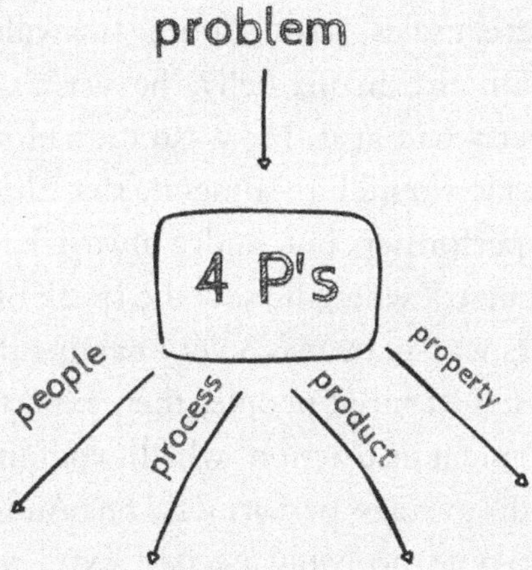

A couple of years ago, I was working with this one very smart man who was a restoration-company owner. We'll call him "Andre." He was a wizard with sales (he was a Jack, for sure!). At this point, I'd begun coaching him, and he had a top-notch brain in many ways—he was willing to take risks, he was a great salesperson, and he could handle delayed gratification.

He called me to ask for some help with a problem at his restoration company. Less than a year before, he'd left his six-figure, corporate job to bootstrap his own restoration company. He was dedicated to achieving a multi-million-dollar valuation as quickly as possible, and he was willing to do whatever it took to get there.

Even though he was used to making $150,000+ at his previous job, he was only taking out about a $40,000 a year salary as the owner of his new restoration business.

He wasn't even twelve months in, when he was already hitting $1 million in revenue (see why this is such an amazing industry?!).

But he did have a big problem—turnover. And if you're an accountant reading this, I don't mean turnover on goods sold. If you're Lebron James reading this, I also don't mean that Andre was fumbling the ball and giving it to the other team. But, in one sense, he was fumbling... with employees.

While he was a great salesperson, optimistic, willing to get his hands dirty, and a man with fire in his belly, he wasn't great with hiring. Honestly, he was pretty bad at it. He wasn't a bad boss, he just wasn't much of a boss at all. He would hire someone that almost any of us could have seen as a poor performer. But Andre always had a double dose of the "entrepreneur's curse," where he saw the speck of gold in the pile of goo. To make matters worse, he was a very hands-off "boss," if you can even call him that. He just hired people, then expected people them to do their job without much instruction, which wouldn't even make sense if he were bringing on average performers, but Andre was hiring *poor* performers. These people probably needed extra attention, and they certainly weren't getting that from Andre. As a result, Andre's employees were constantly walking off the job. I know that at least one became so disgruntled, they slashed someone's tires. (Crazy, right?!)

Now, Andre was facing a problem in his business, of the many you'll face as you grow. And as you do, you need to know how to solve each one. I can tell you how Andre solved his problem—with a new operations manager—but the real issue I want you to zero in, is the understanding of what tools you can use to solve *any* problem.

I call them the 4 Power Tools of Business™ Leaders.

The 4 Power Tools of Business™

I'm a bit of a tech nerd. OK, I'm a huge a tech nerd. Romexterra was one of the first major restorer in our region to use 3D scanning technology!

But the thing is, software and tech are really just *tools*, so instead of saying "I'm a tech nerd," I like to say, "I'm a tools guy," because it makes me feel manly, like Bear Grylls. And in this chapter, we're going to discuss the most important tools of all—the ones you can use to solve any business problem you'll face.

After my heart-to-heart with Andre, he took me up on my advice. He hired an operations manager, and that was a great choice, because using *people* to solve a problem, is one of the 4 Power Tools of Business™ Leaders. But truthfully, that wasn't *the only tool* he had. He had three other major categories of tools he could have used. Here they all are, listed out together:

1) **People:** using your team, subcontractors, or another person to solve your problem

2) **Process:** instruction or enforcing a new or improved procedure, system, or checklist

3) **Product:** this is how you serve your customers, your employees, and your community

4) **Property:** this category includes all your assets: cash, lines of credit, equipment, vans, etc.

Think of these like your four essential tools—like your hammer, screwdriver, tape measure, and ladder (or whatever your four favorite tools are). These are the main tools you have to solve all the problems you're going to face in business.

Quickly consider the major problems you're facing right now:

- Cashflow
- Training
- Marketing

- Expansion
- Collecting money
- Finding employees
- Dealing with insurance agents/companies

For each of these, you can whip out the four tools—people, process, product, and property—and find a fantastic solution.

Have a cashflow problem? You could *hire* someone to do more invoicing, using the people tool. You could also change your process and use the 48-Hour Rule™ more effectively. You could also provide a new "product" to your customers, the insurance companies or the employees involved with invoicing; say you provide a 2 percent discount to the insurers who pay on time, or give a bonus to your employees when they land an invoice within thirty days of the work being done. Finally, you could use an asset, say a new line of credit, to solve your cashflow problem.

The same goes for any problem you face—a quick hack to finding four viable solutions is to list off the four tools and find one to three solutions within each of the four categories. You can even draw it out. Let's say that I was having a problem with employee retention. I could map out the possible solutions just like this:

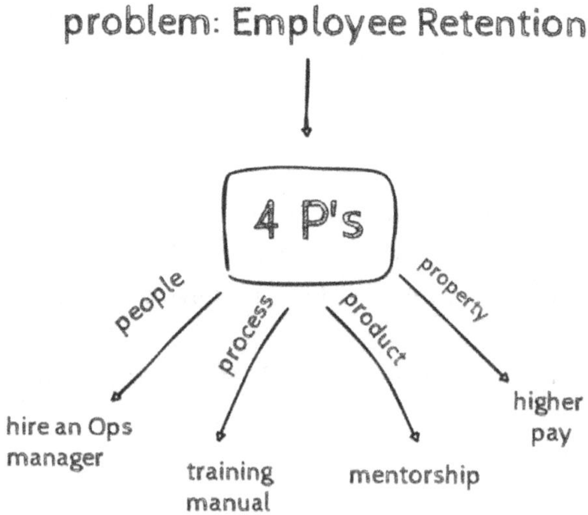

Obviously, I got a little fancy with my drawing, but basically, the important elements to remember are to write the problem, consider the 4 Power Tools, then write out at least one solution for each P.

Pretty simple, right?

That's the gameplan, and it's a simple hack. Now, in the rest of the chapter I'm going to talk about the importance of each of these, but the truth is, if you believe me that these are the four essential ingredients of every company, you could just take my word for it and start solving problems in your business *now.*

But, if you're interested in why these 4 Ps are the key ingredients that allow you to solve any problem, any time, keep reading:

People

Of all the levers a business owner can pull, people goes at the top of the list. As it turns out, *most* of your problems will be *who* problems: who should you hire? Who should you promote? Who could solve this cashflow problem? Who could manage this new project?

When the real-life Jack came to me, one of his biggest problems was his hiring practices and lack of people skills. He could sell a job to anyone, but he had a really big issue keeping employees on board. While his heart was in the right place, coaching and training were not areas he excelled in. I eventually suggested he hire a production manager, one who specialized in coaching and training. Once Jack agreed to the hire and found the right person who excelled in the people skills that Jack was struggling, the business grew from $1.5 million to $5 million in the span of two years.

That's the power of utilizing the people tool correctly.

Process

While people may be the most important tool of all, process is often the most difficult to master. In restoration, your processes include how your teams show up for your clients, the level of efficiency on the job, and how you and your managers lead your teams. Importantly, process also includes things like standard operating procedures, operating manuals or guides, and checklists (typically, all things that George is great with, and things that Jack is not so great with!).

"Product" (AKA: Service)

Ok, we cheated a little with this P. Really, restoration companies are service companies, not product companies, but we had three Ps already, so we just kept going. This category includes all the offerings you provide to your customers.

One service offering that we added for our customers that really helped us stand out was our 3D technology. We were one of the first restoration companies in the region to use a new scanner called a Matterport to do before, during, and after scans of a customer's property. We used this 3D scanner during the sales process, and it really helped win clients over, showing them that we were on the cutting edge of technology in what can often be perceived as a slow industry.

Today, plenty of others use this type of technology, but at the time, we were ahead of the curve.

Property

In the labor business, property, especially the right property, such as the number of trucks, warehouses, and real estate, is essential to operating your business. Sometimes, though, this category can be the quickest drain on one's bank account, especially if they really are a real tools guy!

If you look at my previous example of the Matterport, the device itself could have been classified here.

Typically, when you're solving problems in the restoration business, property can make a material impact in your ability to tackle projects.

- Do you have the right people who share your vision?
- Is your product competitive enough against other restoration companies?
- Are your processes and procedures efficient and repeatable on a large scale?
- Does your property support the scale of business you're projected to do?

You've Already Been Using the 4 Tools

Earlier, in chapter three, we talked about Fishing Holes, the analogy we were using to explain how restorers find new work. You'll remember that we said there are four main ways restoration companies can go to market: online, expansion, new services, or referrals.

If you look at these closely, you'll see that, really, these are the 4 Ps. If you find new work through referrals, you're using people. If you expand your geography, you're using literal property. New services are simply new products. And online marketing, is, essentially, just using a highly specific ad-target process to funnel people toward your organization. So:

- Referrals = people.
- Expansion of geography = property
- New services = product
- Online = process

If that feels like a stretch, let's take the previous example with Andre. He was having a hard time managing his personnel. Ultimately, Andre ended up using "people" to solve his problem (he hired an operations manager). If he'd used "process," one option would have been to create a systematic training manual. He could have used "product," [34] serving his employees differently with more mentorship. Finally, for "property," perhaps he could have raised the compensation levels of each of his employees to create better retainment.

While it may never feel exact, anytime you face a problem in business, if you think of the 4 Ps, you'll be able to come up with four solutions to any issue. The goal isn't to make sure you have four different ideas that fit neatly into the people, process, product, or property categories. Rather, the 4 Power Tools are there to help you quickly get to the most effective, creative solution in any scenario. At a very minimum, by forcing yourself to use the 4 Power Tools, you'll have stopped focusing on the problem, and started focusing on a few viable solutions using different resources. Say you're having a problem with sales—how can you people pull in more sales? Is there a way you can add a new checklist or system to help sales go through faster (process)? Is there a new way you can service your customers (product)? Or, maybe, you can use your physical assets, like technology, to help deals close faster (property)?

You'll find the same opportunities in any area that pops up in your business.

---

[34] Which, again, really means *service* for service-based industries.

Momentum Trigger

Whether you have a $100 million restoration company, or you haven't even started yet, let's solve your next problem now.

Here's what you can do: solve the biggest obstacle you face, right now, with the 4 Power Tools of Business™.

1) Boil down your current biggest obstacle problem.
2) List off a possible solution with each of the 4 Ps.
3) Finally—and this is the clincher!—pick one and do it.

As a couple hacks, remember, it's best to physically use your hand to write all this down. Sounds simple and silly, but writing helps you think more creatively and clearly about the problem and the potential solutions. If you want the cool drawing or just want a little more info about the 4 Power Tools of Business™, go check out RestorationMillionaire.com/resources

Restorer's Recap

- You probably know a lot about tools—that knowledge will help you get started in restoration. But if you want to succeed in the business of restoration, you've got to learn the 4 Power Tools of Business™:
    - People: using your team, subcontractors, or another person to solve your problem
    - Process: instruction or enforcing a new or improved procedure, system, or checklist
    - Product: this is how you serve your customers, your employees, and your community
    - Property: this category includes all your assets; cash, lines of credit, equipment, vans, etc.
- For nearly every problem you face in business, your best solution will come from one of these areas.

CHAPTER 15:
To $8 Million & Beyond

Fishing Hole IV: Add New Services, $5-8 Million
Fishing Hole V: Start New Location, at Fishing Hole I

New Tool

In this chapter, we're going to go over the last two Fishing Holes:

- Fishing Hole I: 1 Service & Online Marketing, $0-1 Million
- Fishing Hole II: Add 1 Referral Source, $1-3 Million
- Fishing Hole III: Add ALL Referral Sources, $3-5 Million
- **Fishing Hole IV: Add New Services, $5-8 Million**
- **Fishing Hole V: Start New Location, at Fishing Hole I**

Fishing Hole IV: Add New Services, $5-8 Million

A few years into our referral program at Romexterra, and my team was rocking it—we had marketers on our team specifically hired to connect with our insurance agents every two weeks on a rotating basis. It worked like a charm. With our claims screening process that we were offering, agents thought the world of us—they were calling us like crazy to go to homeowner's homes. Our team was looking at everything, from cat-pee stains to crazy fire damage. We would land a ton of work this way and *save* a ton of work for the local insurance agents.

Meanwhile, a hailstorm came through the Chicagoland area that we serviced, and the hail damaged tons of roofs. Roofs were outside our service offerings, so we didn't take much notice, at first. But then, the insurance agents that we'd built relationships with started calling us:

"Hey Romexterra! A ton of unknown door-knockers started going through the neighborhoods that were hit most heavily by the storms. Our policyholders are calling us asking who *we trust* to fix their roofs... We trust you—can you also do roofs?"

"Hey Alex! Does your team also do roofing? We'd love to be able to refer you, because we trust you, and our homeowners are getting a little nervous with these newer roofing companies."

"Hello! When will y'all start doing roofing? We'd love to be able to refer you after that last hailstorm... "

We were getting a call from every Flo, Jake, and Gecko in the insurance industry. Finally, I decided it was time: "Heck with it! Let's do roofing!"

I actually did the first few roof inspections on my own, signed the damaged ones, met with the adjusters, and boom, we were in the roofing business.

We knew hardly anything about roofing. But, I had plenty of friends in the roofing industry whom I could call, and I knew I'd have several weeks before the jobs needed to be completed. So, I called up my contacts, got some pointers on all things roofing—they told me what I'd need, general timelines, who the best roofing subcontractors were in the area.

A few weeks after I jumped on my first roof, and Romexterra was working on our first roofs. By the end of the quarter, we'd added about $1 million of additional roofing work!

When Your Referral Partners Work for You

It's amazing how much of the work your referrals partners will do for you, after you've built up a trustworthy reputation and found out what's important to them. Because we'd solved the insurance agents' biggest pain point—helping their customers with their claims so they didn't cancel their policies—the insurance agents wanted and needed us. We didn't even plan on getting into roofing—our partners *pushed* us to!

When your referral partners trust you so much that they're begging you to open up a new service, you're doing something right. Plus, when someone else markets you, the way the agents were marketing us to the homeowners, selling is a cinch: we weren't going to homes as unknown door-knockers offering a "free roof inspection" the way most roofing companies were. We were *invited* into homes and onto roofs, as trusted partners.

You see how simple that is? Once you've built out the referral partner network, and you've proven your trustworthiness, there's almost nothing you can't sell through that network. That's why I have "add new services" as Fishing Hole *four,* which comes only *after* you've built out a fantastic referral program, and duplicated it as much as possible to every referral source

Once you've maximized online marketing and created a world-class referral program that you've systemized for all your referral sources in the industry (insurance agents, plumbers property managers, etc.), you'll already be making millions in revenue. But just like every other Fishing Hole, you'll eventually hit your point of diminishing returns, even with referrals. Then, it's time to add on new services, and, eventually, expand into a new territory.

So, in this final chapter, we're going to go over the final two Fishing Holes:

- Fishing Hole I: 1 Service & Online Marketing, $0-1 Million
- Fishing Hole II: Add 1 Referral Source, $1-3 Million
- Fishing Hole III: Add ALL Referral Sources, $3-5 Million
- **Fishing Hole IV: Add New Services, $5-8 Million**
- **Fishing Hole V: Start New Location, at Fishing Hole I**

We'll start by unpacking Fishing Hole IV: Add New Services before moving on to the final hole.

Let's get fishing.

Adding Services: The Easy Bolt-On

If you've been following the Restoration Millionaire Method™ to this point, adding on services may be one of the easiest new holes you dive into, at least at first. The same way that Romexterra was primed and ready to add services to our business, you will be, too.

For one, you'll already be halfway there: In the same way that your referral partners simply just need to know that you provide additional services, your online marketing that's already rocking from Fishing Hole one, needs some very simple updates. Add a few changes on your website which will already be on lock step, and you'll simply need to update your website, change your ads a little, and voila—you have new jobs flowing in.

Secondly, you're already in the door with homeowners: Many restorers, if not most, start in either water mitigation, emergency services, or some other niche that allows them to get through the front door. Once a homeowner lets you in to fix a leaky sink, repair a damaged wall, pull out moldy carpet, or rebuild a wall after a fire, the only question is, "Can you also do. . ?"

Particularly when there's been a fire or water damage that requires a rebuild, the homeowner will want you to do all the additional work other than the initial emergency work. In fact, I've found that the more services you provide beyond the emergency work, the easier it is to land the emergency work. Say you show up to a house that's recently had a fire and water damage because of the sprinklers. If you tell them that you can handle the water mitigation, the fire clean-out, *and* the rebuild, it's so much less stress on the homeowner to only have to work with one company that they know and trust.

When it is time to add new services, you'll be surprised how many more yesses you'll hear on emergency work, just because you can do the rebuild or reconstruction as well.

Referral partners have much the same attitude as homeowners—once they trust you, it's easier and feels safer to use you as opposed to an unknown entity. Again, that's why you niche at first, as much as possible—it gives you the opportunity to become world-class at one particular service area, then systemize it so you can consistently deliver that high-quality work.

New Services -- Easy to Sell, Harder To Do

While new services are easy to add on and easy to sell, there are a few caveats. Particularly, doing the actual work can create new difficulties.

First, for all my restorers who started in emergency services, fire rebuilds, and other types of reconstruction are much more complex. You can't whip in and out like you did with water mitigation and quick cleanups. Be prepared for quite the learning curve.

Secondly, you'll notice quickly that profit margins on rebuilds and reconstruction are much less than quick, easy jobs. Reconstruction requires more manpower, and there are more material costs as well. While total profit may be up, your *margins* may actually go down when you add on new services, particularly if you're adding on more complex, labor-intensive work.

You'll also need new managers to oversee the new line of business. When I hopped up on those first few roofs, I handled the inspections and insurance claims personally. Pretty quickly, we had plenty of new work coming in (thanks to the hailstorm), so I had to develop some systems to organize this new line of business, build out some new SOPs, and eventually hire a new department manager who had more experience in roofing. If you're adding on a similar new service, you'll need your own SOPs, new leaders, separate crews, and probably new equipment.

This is when having a fantastic technological platform can *really* come in handy. When you're operating at a high level in an area you have expertise in, you *may* be able to get away with fewer technological tools, organizational skills, and SOPs. If you've been doing water mitigation work, you know, roughly, what needs to be done, when, *and* you also have all the numbers "ballparked" in your head—you can quickly guestimate the profit margin on a job based off a few simple factors. But once you step into a new arena, your knowledge doesn't apply. Sure, you could spend *months* learning about everything, but if you've been following the Restoration Millionaire Method™, you'll have work coming in so quickly, you'll want a technology platform that can help you keep your job flows organized and your profit margins in check. (May I suggest, ahem, *Albiware?!)*

Since we're talking about profit margins, let's also discuss two other numbers that can shift rapidly when you open a new service in your restoration business: CAC and managerial expenses.

CAC Keeps Coming Back

Remember, CAC means "Customer acquisition cost." Remember, back in chapter three, I suggested always aiming to keep your CAC at around 15 percent, with a maximum of 20 percent. That's important when you're adding new services, because of the shifting profit margins. Let me explain:

When you jump from online marketing into referrals, your goal is to make sure your total, blended CAC stays below 20 percent. It may try to inch up above that, because you may be *spending money* on your referral program.

When you add on new services, you won't technically be spending much more money on marketing (although you will be spending quite a bit more on managers and new equipment). You'll just be shifting the conversation with homeowners, referral sources, and online marketing enough to account for your new offerings. That doesn't really cost more, but, when you add on a new service, your CAC can change, because new offerings are worth a different amount. So, if $10,000 in ads was bringing in $60,000 of work, if you add on a new service, the value of that work could shift; fires are worth more, emergency services are worth the least, roofing is somewhere in between. You may be getting the same amount of leads with your budget, but those leads may be worth more (or less).

Just follow the rule of thumb here: Aim for a 15-percent CAC at all times.

New-Manager Sticker Shock

When you first start a new line of business or add on a new service, you'll probably need to make some investment into new hires, new equipment, new trucks, more warehouse space, etc., which means, your *overall* non-marketing expenses *will* temporarily go through the roof. Particularly, you're likely to need a new department manager. And you don't want to skimp on these.

While I was working with one of my restoration coaching clients, they came to a point where they needed to hire a fantastic manager for an area of their business. They found one, but they wanted to bring him on as a "test" hire for a few months and pay him $20 an hour. This person was worth well into the six figures, and there's no way they would have worked for that price. My coaching client was about to sabotage their growth because they had sticker shock.

When you're adding on a new service, know that you'll likely need to invest in a manager for that department. These are *not* cheap, but they're worth it. If you've been following the fishing-hole method we've suggested, by now, when you add on a new service, you'll likely have overnight growth. That's good, for revenue reasons, but it also means you're going to have a ton of net-new work in an area you likely have very little expertise in. Invest in an experienced manager who knows all about your new service offering. Trust me—You'll be happy you did.

Georges! Don't sabotage growth by trying to save money on new hires, especially when you're trying to open a new service. Likely you'll need an experienced manager to oversee your new service area, and these *will cost you* upfront. That's OK!

Turn the Lights On

Once you've managed to crack online marketing *and* referrals, turning on a new service is like turning on the lights after you've figured out the electricity—once the groundwork has been laid, the rest is a piece of cake.

That's why I suggest staying focused early on, until it's time to diversify your offerings. By the time you've mined online marketing and referrals for all the money you can, adding on a new service will be a breeze, and, nearly instantly, you'll make more money, just by telling the world about your new offering.

***

Now, that's Fishing Hole IV. You ready to discuss Fishing Hole number five?!

- Fishing Hole I: 1 Service & Online Marketing, $0-1 Million
- Fishing Hole II: Add 1 Referral Source, $1-3 Million
- Fishing Hole III: Add ALL Referral Sources, $3-5 Million
- Fishing Hole IV: Add New Services, $5-8 Million
- **Fishing Hole V: Start New Location, at Fishing Hole I**

Fishing Hole V: Start New Location, at Fishing Hole I

There are a couple reasons I save adding on a new location for last in the Restoration Millionaire Method™. In some ways it's the hardest way to add revenue, because you'll likely need a new satellite office, and you'll almost certainly need new crews, new managers, etc. In other ways, though, I save this lesson for last. You see, if you've mastered everything else we've been discussing—the "hard skills," such the 48-Hour Rule™, SOPs, CIRCLS, WALT, etc., along with the leadership skills such as, Hiring, Firing, and Inspiring, Dreaming in 4D, learning to be proactive, etc.—you just need to open a new location, and do it all over again. Only this time, you're a pro, you have more cash to invest upfront, and you have a trusted relationship with employees, customers, and the market.

Author Brian Tracy once said that "The first million is hard, but the second million is inevitable." If you're following the focused-fishing-holes method we've been discussing, you'll find this truth to be self-evident; business, by nature, is typically difficult. But once you've setup one headquarters, mastered it to $8 million or more by utilizing SOPs, organization, and people, opening a new satellite office is pretty objective: open a new location, start with one service and online marketing, and then scale through the entire Restoration Millionaire Method™ again with that new location.

Technically, the Restoration Millionaire Method™ suggests staying with one location until you've hit $8 million or more. In reality, it's not about the numbers—you may need to expand earlier, or later, depending on your area. The goal throughout the Restoration Millionaire Method™ is to keep track of diminishing returns. At every Fishing Hole, you want to ask yourself, "If I add more effort into this Fishing Hole, will I keep reaping a worthwhile benefit?" If you can keep fishing from a hole with increased effort and catching plenty of more fish, then, you have *not* hit the point of diminishing returns. But, if you were to add more time, effort, money, or manpower, for little or *no* additional gain, then, that hole is tapped, and you need to keep fishing there, keeping your efforts steady, but going elsewhere to find new fish.

A technical way of answering the question of "have I hit diminishing returns?" is to look at your CAC on a per-Fishing Hole basis. If your CAC for a given Fishing Hole is 15 percent at a $10,000 investment, will it stay at 15 percent if you add on an additional $5,000? Or, suddenly, is your CAC for that Fishing Hole going to shoot up to 25 percent or more? Every Fishing Hole has a point at which additional effort won't yield too many more results, so you'll need to fish elsewhere for more fish.

When it comes to adding on a new location, depending on the population size of your original area, you may hit this point at $8 million in revenue, or it could be much later. The point is, when you know you've maxed out, online marketing, referrals, and new services, it's time to open a new office.

How to Open a New Location

A new location is pretty simple in concept—it's going to require everything you first needed when you started out:

What You Will Need in a New Location:

- A crew
- A manager
- An office and/or storage facility
- Some start-up cash
- Online marketing
- A truck
- Other supplies

If you bootstrapped like me, you didn't have everything on that list when you started your restoration company. I've known a ton of retirees—most of us just started showing up at people's houses asking if we could dry their carpets or repair their burned down walls; once we got the rare "yes," we went to Home Depot or Lowe's to rent the tools we needed!

That sort of bootstrapping creativity is needed to start that first location, but luckily, you won't need that for your second spot. Instead, you can just buy what you need to get going. You will need most of the list I suggest above, *but* you won't need:

- New website
- New software
- Office manager
- Accountant
- Dispatchers
- Other back-of-house staff
- Silly first-time mistakes!

All the back-of-house staff, such as administrators, dispatchers, accountants, bookkeepers, etc., you won't need again.

So, what many restorers do is they have one main headquarters that houses all the back-of-house staff and some of the largest equipment then, a smaller "satellite office," where the production manager and the crew for the new area can meet-up at (this is also the place to store the trucks and/or certain equipment).

Start at Fishing Hole I & Organizational Chart 1

Notice I *don't* suggest you take every service from your first location and replicate it into your second one. Rather, the Restoration Millionaire Method™ suggests you *start back over* with Fishing Hole I: 1 Service & Online Marketing.

At your new location, you'll have all that focused power that helped you scale into the millions with your original location. Don't worry—with your second location, going through the Fishing Holes will go much, much quicker.

As far as your organizational chart, you'll follow the same path as before:

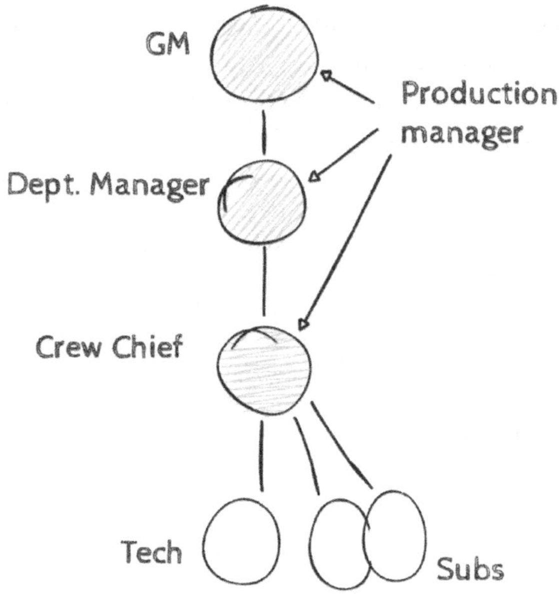

Only, this time, "you" will be a production manager. Because they won't have *any* of the back-of house responsibilities and they'll be able to work with you and your experienced team, copy SOPs from your headquarters, and benefit from all the know-how and war stories of everyone at your headquarters, this second office should do very well.

Where To Open the Next Location?

For your first location, I suggest drawing about a thirty to sixty-minute circle outside of your central office, and staying within that circle, that way you can really get to know all the referral partners in your locality, and you and your crews aren't driving to Timbuktu every time to do a new job.

For your second location, you have options, but a great idea is to make it about an hour to an hour and a half away from your first office—not so far where you can't cross-utilize your staff if absolutely necessary but not so close that you aren't maximizing the new territory.

And, when you're talking about opening up a new location... it's all about, well*, location, location.*

In this context, I want you to think about one term:

Population center.

Everything in restoration hinges on some fairly steady percentages of homeowners making insured claims on their home every year. So, when you're picking where your new location is going to be, you want to pick an area that maximizes your opportunity for restoration work. Generally, the denser an area is with owned homes, the more money you have available for restoration. So, you want to pick an area for your next location that allows you to add the maximum amount of new work. I have a really, really simple tool at RestorationMillion.com/resources that will allow you to plug in some quick numbers and get an estimate for how much restoration work is available in any area, that way you can play around with some different numbers until you find a location that maximizes the potential of your new office (and, I have the tool broken down by category, so it can also help you decide which service you want to provide first).

Generally speaking, you can estimate about $200-$300 of restoration work per year, per person. That equates to about $2 – 3 million of restoration work opportunity every year for every 10,000 people![35]

Full-Circle With Set, Prove, Rep

Notice that the whole idea of adding that final Fishing Hole is this:

Set, Prove, Rep.

It's almost like we came full-circle back to where we started... on purpose!

---

35 "Facts + Statistics: Homeowners and Renters Insurance." III. Accessed November 28, 2023; Bureau, US Census. "Historical Households Tables." Census.gov, November 21, 2023.

With your first location, you're setting the foundation first and proving the model. You're using *Set, Prove, Rep,* at various areas of your business—you're trying out SOPs, iterating on them, then replicating them. You're trying out referrals with one source, proving that it works, then expanding to every other referral source. Now, when it's time to add on a new location, on a larger level, you're using Set, Prove, Rep to add on that new location. You've already set the foundation with your first location. Then, you've iterated on it to prove that that model works. Now, it's time to *replicate & scale* across the globe! (Ok, maybe not across the globe, but at least across your region, and maybe, across the country).

In fact, that's what we've really been discussing in this whole book.

There's a lot in here—over 60,000 words of information for you and your team to make it as a millionaire in restoration. Maybe you don't remember everything the first time you go through, but the basic premises should stick: Set, Prove, Rep, is probably one of the easiest to remember. And this three-step idea holds true in the small ways, and in the macro-level as well.

Also, don't forget about the two brains of business: The jacks and the Georges. Likely, you're more one than the other. You're either a "Jack of all trades," who's fantastic at selling, loves action, and forgets the details. Or, you're a George—the steady, true, often kind leader who thinks of all the ways in and out of a situation before you take action.

All my Jacks need to know—you're a visionary, and if you slow down, just a tad, you'll be able to sprinkle in some of the George details you're missing. You can do that with SOPs, learning, or people—can hire more Georges in your business, you can get a mentor (or devour books, podcasts, and other material) that helps hold up a mirror to your flaws so you can fill them in, or finally, you can also add in systems, procedures, checklists, and technology that helps align your business with the most important goals so you don't have to get caught up in those details. Again, may I suggest the best platform ever created (although I'm a little biased!) for restorers, Albiware!

George—you have a different set of strengths. You know how to operate with great efficiency, and organization. Your warehouse is probably immaculately organized. You probably have a system for everything in your company. There are few Is and Ts that you don't dot or cross. Insurance agents, customers, and employees love you. You just need to add in some Jack-magic that brings in the sales. For you, consider reading some books on salesmanship, or hiring plenty of Jacks that can help scale your business. Again, books, podcasts, and other content can really help you fill in the missing gaps here. And I *know* that all my Georges love a good system, so I'll add in the same plug I did for Jack: check out Albiware. It's built by restorers, for restorers.

Momentum Trigger

I want you to decide what your next service offering will be, *even if* you're not ready for it. Imagining it and visualizing it can be powerful. So, let's go find your next new service.

To find your new service, you need to answer three questions:

- What would be the *easiest* service to offer?
- What new service would make the most *revenue*?
- What service are my customers and/or referral sources *already asking* me to perform?

After brainstorming the above questions, write down your new service. If you're ready to implement it, go checkout RestorationMillionaire.com/resources to find SOPs, and tips and tricks on each additional type of service. If you aren't quite there yet, write down that new service offering and visualize how successful it will be, *soon.*

Once you've added new services, and you've maximized every revenue opportunity within your main location, it's time to open a new location, at Fishing Hole I.

Restorer's Recap

- After you've built trust within your network using a systemized referral program, your referral sources will often come to you, nearly *begging* you to add new services.
- It's much easier for restorers to start with one service until they've developed enough systems that they can provide world-class service, repeatedly, at scale. This allows you to build trust with your customers, so that later, you can add new offerings.
- While new services are often easy to bolt-on top your existing marketing strategy, they often add unforeseen headaches: new services can be harder to perform, require new management and SOPs, and often take much longer than emergency services to complete.
- Instead of trying to penny-pinch, when you start a new service offering, *hire a manager* who has experience in that area. Recognize an experienced, excellent manager will *not* be cheap.
- Once you've maximized *all other* Fishing Holes, meaning your online marketing, your referral programs, and your services are running smoothly and bringing in maximum revenue, it's time to add a new location, starting again at Fishing Hole I.

CONCLUSION:
The Only Metric You'll Ever Need

In business, everyone seems to have the "one metric" or the "few" that matter: KPIs, revenue, profit, profit margin... these are all important, but there's only *one* that I think matters more than all the others:

Momentum.

In the end, the element that will decide whether your business makes it into the stars that you're shooting for, is momentum.

Momentum may be hard to define on a balance sheet, but you know when you have it—when you walk into the office, and there's a swell of energy every day, where employees are excited to execute, numbers are going up, and there's a general air of pride in one's work, you have momentum. Compare that to the humdrum feeling of "working my nine to five," that many people have, and it's easy to see what momentum is, and what it's not.

Momentum builds upon itself—a small amount of excitement in one area of a business ignites passion in another, which continues to build: A crew finishes a huge job, and they thank the sales and marketing team for bringing in the lead. The sales and marketing team thanks the referral source for the introduction. At each touchpoint, the ball of momentum grows. Over time, if that same energy persists, the entire organization builds more and more momentum until it becomes *unstoppable.*

Momentum is a must for a small company—without the resources, manpower, and expertise of a large-scale enterprise, a small company relies on the hopeful expectations of its employees and customers. But momentum at a *large company?* There's almost nothing that a large company with momentum can't achieve. That's why companies like Apple, Disney, Microsoft, Netflix, Facebook, and others continue to win. They have achieved mass *and* speed[36], the two major components that physicists use to define momentum mathematically.

I want the same for you. I want you to walk into the office every day, with an ever-increasing promise of more and more momentum. I want your teammates to see you and feel inspired. I want your sales team to sell more. I want your employees to go home happy to see their families, and happy to come into the work the next day because they know they're building something, together, that has momentum. If you can continue to stoke the fires of momentum as your company scales in size, you will be unstoppable—a force that not only has the excitement and hope of a better tomorrow, but one that has the resources to tackle bigger and bigger problems, and jobs.

We've talked about a lot in this book on restoration—SOPs, referral programs, CAC—but the truth is, one metric will rule them all. *Momentum.*

It's hard to define, easy to feel. Few companies have it, but those that do, often change the world. That may sound like a tall order for a "small restoration company," but get this:

Restoration is the industry that puts people's homes and lives back together. In restoration, you have the opportunity to give hard workers that many look down upon—such as immigrants or those with less formal education – the chance at making an excellent living doing something they can be proud of.

When hurricane Irma shook Florida, my team sent a truckload of goods to help out those impacted. When COVID-19 rocked the world, my team worked with our fire department to offer free COVID cleanings. When our employees couldn't understand the complex paperwork to purchase a home, we helped them. These may seem small to you, but, like momentum, these small acts that a restoration company can perform build, like momentum. And more importantly, a job for an

---

[36] Technically, it's mass and *velocity,* which is speed *in the same direction.*

employee, a rebuilt home, or a well-deserved promotion, can build momentum in an individual, and open their eyes to greater possibilities.

When I was a teenager, a kind businessman offered me his extra truck and snowplow to help me get into business as a snow-blower. That was a small bit of energy he inserted into my life. A couple years later my father and I went into business together at Romexterra, another momentum injection. A few years after that, I turned Romexterra over to my father, so my cofounder and I could build the world's first technology platform (Albi) dedicated to solving the problems inherent to the restoration industry.

The momentum that first businessman started, with a simple snowplow, hasn't stopped. It's spread. I don't anticipate Albi as my final stop. I have more to make, and my employees will hopefully do even better things.

Momentum's like that—it multiplies and builds.

With this book, if I've given you nothing else, I hope I've given you *your* first little snowplow, a nudge, a push, a bit of energy into your next move. Maybe you're making $10 million in revenue BUT you picked this book up to fix your CAC problem—I hope the tools I gave you were just the little extra momentum you needed. Maybe you're at $500,000 and you didn't know what to do next. I hope you found the momentum you need with the Restoration Millionaire Method™ to pick up more steam, make more sales, and keep building the company of your dream. If you weren't even sure that restoration was the industry for you, I hope you are, now.

It's a dream industry.

The first thing you need to do, is start, now. What's your next step, the next move that will help you build some momentum in your business, or even in your life? Remember, momentum compound—if you can start building a little momentum today, you'll be able to build more tomorrow.

Whatever that one thing is that you can do to create the most forward momentum in your business, your team, or your life, go do it *now.*

Your employees, your community, your business, is waiting for you.

And if you ever need my help, Albi and I will be here for you. Go drop us a line at RestorationMillionaire.com/resources.

Go build the company of your dreams.

#GoCrush

ACKNOWLEDGEMENTS:

To Nick and Daniela Duta, my wonderful parents, for always supporting me and giving me the privilege of the American dream. I know it was incredibly hard to break away from the status quo. You made incredible sacrifices. I'm super grateful for the incredible life lessons your struggles have taught me.

To my brother David who's making me incredibly proud by doing everything, **better.**

To Laura Duta, my beautiful, incredible, supporting wife. Thank you for never saying "no" to any of my craziest dreams or ambitions. From day one, you've put up with too many of our dates being interrupted by emergency service calls, and you've allowed "quality time" to happen while we were on moving trucks. Thank you for always accepting me for who I am.

To my entire book team who made this happen. Paul, my writing partner, Timmy, the mastermind behind all of the designs, and Wakeema, Kayla, and Miranda. Oh, and Michele, for making sure that I don't get cancelled.

Special thanks to Ricelli Mordecai, Jeff Moore, and Ben Surdi for all your input during this process.

To Matt Bando, the first person who believed in me and fueled my entrepreneurial spirit when I was only sixteen.

To my entire family at Romexterra, current and past team members, who believed in the crazy dream and taught me so many lessons I get to share with readers today. Marie, Jose, Vinnie, Jason, Igor, Irina, Omar, Jackie, Greg, and so many others.

To Oscar, our crew chief at Romexterra who always had ambitions of climbing the restoration ladder; however, you're no longer with us. ☹

To everyone at Albiware joining us on the mission to propel restoration forward. Joining a startup and pushing to the limits is no easy task.

To Shamoil, the cofounder of Albiware, for believing in this crazy mission of innovating in this industry that's so near and dear to my heart.

To Abby, my executive assistant who keeps me sane.

To Joey and Henry, our amazing board members at Albiware, who believed in us when no one else did.

To all of my coaching clients, who have taught me so much about how to explain and teach frameworks, who are making me proud by changing their own lives. To Joe, Alex, Marin, Gerald, Bob, John, and Brandon.

To all of my coaches, trainers, and mentors who have poured their wisdom into me. Thank you, Bill Prosch, Dan Martell, Stephanie Karlovitz, Clate Mask, Sara & Tyler Reynolds.

WATER MITIGATION SOP:

Read the full SOP here or download it at:
RestorationMillionaire.com/resources

albi

Your Restoration Company

Emergency Services Department

Standard Operating Procedures

The Emergency Services Department (ESRV) Standard Operating Procedures (SOP) aims to standardize the workflow for Emergency Services projects, eliminating unnecessary confusion and stress. The ESRV department manager will enforce the protocol of the ESRV SOP along with the General Manager.

Roles needed to satisfy the SOP:

- Call Taker (anyone within the company)
- Dispatcher (Administrative Department)
- Emergency Services Project Manager
- Emergency Services Crew Chief
- Emergency Services Technician
- Accounts Receivable Specialist
- Office Admin (Administrative Department)
- Facility Manager

Lead Qualification

The Call Taker receives all phone calls and determines qualified leads. The qualifications must include all of the following:

1) The customer needs an emergency service provided by the company (YOUR SERVICES). This includes any repairs when appropriate.
2) The customer is within an **X-mile** radius of **Your Address**
3) The customer identifies themselves as the homeowner or authorized by the homeowner.
4) The customer is willing to allow **YOUR COMPANY** to perform a property inspection of the damages before giving a price.

The Call Taker promises the customer that a project manager will arrive on the scene within the "lead time" on the dispatch board. This "lead time" is set by the Dispatcher. From that moment forward, the project manager will assist from there.

The Call Taker inputs information into the dispatch board. The information should include the following:

- First and Last Name
- Phone Number
- Email Address
- (Property Address, street, city, state, zip code)
- Call Taker's initials & time
- Call description (Make sure to identify customer pain points and what they are looking for and see how you could be a good fit)
- Appointment window
- Referral source (It's always important to keep track of where qualified leads are coming from; this can ultimately help your marketing team determine which target areas work)

The call taker notifies dispatch as soon as the call comes in. If your company uses Albi, they can input all the information above, including the call description note and dispatch notification, into a project in Albi.

Pro Tip: If a call comes in after business hours and is a mold loss or a non-active leak that has been sitting for 72 hours or more, your company should promise the client a 2-hour appointment window during the next business day.

***Business days are considered **YOUR COMPANY'S BUSINESS DAYS.**

Dispatch

The Dispatcher copies information from the Dispatch board to the ESRV board under the assigned project manager and dispatches the Project Manager within 10 minutes of receiving notification of a lead.

The Project Manager confirms they received the information and hit the road within 20 minutes of dispatch. The Project Manager informs dispatch of the arrival on site. (Dispatchers should already be aware of this without being told through GPS or dash cams.)

3 | Water Mitigation SOP | www.albiware.com

Sale

The Project Manager performs a full inspection of the property. The Project Manager determines if insurance coverage exists and executes the sale. The ESRV Work Authorization is presented to the customer without charge if insurance coverage exists and there are no limits. An estimate is written and delivered to the customer if limits are present. In the absence of insurance coverage, the work will be priced and documented on the work authorization. The PM collects half or the total amount of the initial upfront deposit and sends an email to billing with the work authorization and agreed amount.

The Project Manager performs a Matterport scan of the property, including non-affected continuous areas. The Project Manager uploads the loss description into Albi and notifies dispatch of the sale, obtains ETA for the crew, confirms time with the client, and sends a loss description over to dispatch as well as necessary resources. If you're an Albi user, you can pull this precise information to place on your job board.

The Project Manager Updates notes can also be found in Albi, which include dates and estimated revenue. If possible, the Project Manager should wait on site for crews to arrive and walk crews through the scope of the scene.

The Project Manager is responsible for following up with a client every 24 to 72 hours until the project sells if an estimate was given, the project did not sell. The project is marked as a "no sale" and is closed by the ESRV manager if no sale is made. Two weeks and at least three cold follow-ups later, the project is closed.

If there's no sale, the PM needs to scope out the scene and conduct a PRE-MIT SCAN. If the customer does not have an email, the PM should send the paperwork to the customer before scheduling.

If no work is to be performed on the project by YOUR COMPANY, it is marked "no estimate." If a project only needs an outside source (i.e., a plumber) and cannot be handled in-house, the PM calls dispatch to refer to the job and marks "no estimate."

If another department is needed immediately for a project, dispatch is informed to call them in.

When environmental hazards occur on a job site, instruct crews to stabilize and not touch potential hazardous material until dispatch can perform environmental testing/abatement. (Pre 1984).

Pro Tip: The minimum companywide trip charge is **YOUR COMPANYWIDE**

CHARGE.

Production: These are just some to the steps you can take depending on which category your crew is working on.

CATEGORY 1

1. The Crew Chief performs an initial inspection of the property with the homeowner or (Agent in care). The Crew Chief signs work authorization and begins the Matterport scan if the PM has not yet done so. Once that's completed, the Crew Chief takes a full photo of the report.
2. The Crew Chief informs technicians of their findings from the initial inspection and any PPE necessities or hazards in the area.
3. Set up damage containment barriers (if necessary). Install protective flooring to cover and protect the area that is affected.

Pro Tip: If you need to remove the carpet, put a roll of carpet on the driveway leading to the truck, so dust doesn't track outside. If that's not an option, then use rosin paper.

4. If a homeowner has any allergies or sensitivities to dust, AFD is placed and runs during the job and the drying process. If you use Albi, this is something essential to put in a note for ALL crew members to see.
5. If surface water is greater than ½", install submersible pumps. If not, skip this step.
6. Dehumidifiers are placed on the job and begin running.
7. Extract the water from the affected areas. Use a hard surface wand for hard surfaces and a carpet wand for the carpet. The extractor is hooked to a garden hose and pumped into a toilet or outside. Only Cat 1 and Cat 2 water may be pumped outside.
8. Material is manipulated out of affected areas and covered and protected.
9. Lift the carpet using a carpet awl. Then test it for delamination. Once the carpet is delaminated, it's documented and removed.
10. Tiles (vinyl or ceramic) can be protected and saved if the wood subfloor can be dried from underneath. If not, the crew must remove the tiles to dry the subfloor. If the tiles are on a concrete subfloor, they are dried with added heat. If tiles are not popping or showing distress in grout lines, you should still attempt to dry them.
11. If it's hardwood flooring- make sure to extract the water. The purpose of this is to protect and save the flooring. Install Injectidry and hook the water extractor to Injectidry mats before running the system. LGR must be present, and the hardwood floor is preferably tented with poly.
12. Remove laminate/ engineered wood flooring as well as any underlayment.

5 | Water Mitigation SOP | www.albiware.com

13. Interior walls: Remove baseboards, drill wall holes, and point air movers into the wall.
14. Exterior walls: If the insulation is wet, flood and cut the walls. Also, make sure to remove the insulation. If it's dry, apply the same steps as the interior walls.
15. Cabinetry/Vanities: If it's on interior walls, drill holes in the toe kick as well as the interior of the cabinet. After you complete this step, install cavity drying systems. Cabinets are detached to remove wet drywall.
16. Ceilings: Wet ceilings are cut out due to the hazard of the ceiling potentially falling unless there is less than ten sq ft of mild saturation in the ceiling (use your best judgment)
17. Plaster: Plaster follows the same protocol. However, you need to insert the heat to dry it and add dry chambers.
18. Once you remove the affected materials, conduct a thorough cleaning and removal of the impacted area. Make sure to remove unnecessary floor protection. HEPA Vacuuming will occur on every job.
19. Apply Antimicrobial to affected areas.
20. Place drying equipment per IICRC regulations. (1 air mover per every room, 1 AM per every 50-75 sqft of floor space and up to 2' high on walls, 1 air mover for every 150 sqft of the ceiling and wall space above 2' high, 1 air mover per each offset greater than 18". CF of air is divided by 50 to achieve the AHAM pints needed for dehu. Large DHM 135 AHAM regular size Dehu 70 AHAM).
21. After the work is complete (the post mitigation Matterport Scan is complete). Crew Chiefs remove any unnecessary protection. They also conduct a final walk-through with the clients, explaining their work in detail.
22. The Crew Chief sets up a date for equipment to be picked up with the client and calls dispatch to notify the date set. The Crew Chief asks dispatch if there is trash to be picked up that didn't fit in the truck and notates the information in the file.

CATEGORY 2

1. The Crew Chief performs an initial inspection of the property with the homeowner. If the PM has not done so, the Crew Chief signs a work authorization and performs the Matterport scan. The Crew Chief takes a full photo report.
2. The Crew Chief informs technicians of findings from the initial inspection and any PPE necessities or hazards in the area.
3. Damage containment barriers are set up (if necessary). Install floor protection to cover and protect the floor leading to the affected area. Pro Tip: When the carpet needs to be removed, put a roll of carpet on the driveway leading to the truck, so dust doesn't track outside. If that's not an option, then use rosin paper.
4. If a homeowner has any allergies or sensitivities to dust, AFD is placed and runs during the job and drying process.
5. If surface water is greater than ½", submersible pumps are installed. If not, skip this step.
6. Dehumidifiers are placed on the job and begin running.
7. Extract water from the affected areas. Use a hard surface wand for hard surfaces and a carpet wand for carpets. The extractor is hooked to a garden hose and pumps into a toilet or outside. Only Cat 1 and Cat 2 water may be pumped outside.
8. Material is manipulated out of affected areas and covered and protected.
9. Lift the carpet using a carpet awl. Then test it for delamination. Once the carpet is delaminated, it will be removed. Otherwise, the crew will lift the carpet and the pad removed.
10. Tiles (vinyl or ceramic) are covered, protected, and saved if the wood subfloor can be dried from underneath. If not, remove the tiles to dry the subfloor.
11. Hardwood Flooring- flooring is removed.
12. Remove Laminate/ Engineered wood flooring and underlayment.
13. Interior walls: Remove Baseboards, drill the wall holes, and inject air into the wall.
14. Exterior walls: If the insulation is wet, flood and cut the walls. Also, make sure to remove the insulation. If it's dry, apply the same steps as the interior walls.
15. Cabinetry/Vanities: If you're working on interior walls, drill holes in the toe kick as well as the interior of the cabinet. If it's exterior walls, cabinets are detached to remove wet drywall.
16. Ceilings: Cut out any due to the hazard of the ceiling potentially falling

7 | Water Mitigation SOP | www.albiware.com

17. Plaster: The plaster follows the same protocol. However, you need to insert heat to dry it and add dry chambers.
18. After removing the damaged materials, thoroughly clean the floor and remove all unnecessary floor coverings.
19. Apply Antimicrobial to affected areas.
20. Place drying equipment per IICRC regulations. (1 air mover per every room, 1 AM per every 50-75 sqft of floor space and up to 2' high on walls, 1 air mover for every 150 sqft of the ceiling and wall space above 2' high, 1 air mover per each offset greater than 18". CF of air is divided by 50 to achieve the AHAM pints needed for dehu. Large DHM 135 AHAM regular size Dehu 70 AHAM).
21. After the work is complete, (the post mitigation Matterport Scan is complete) Crew Chiefs remove any unnecessary protection. They also conduct a final walk through with the clients, explaining their work in detail.
22. The Crew Chief sets up a date for equipment to be picked up with the client and calls dispatch to notify the date set. The Crew Chief asks dispatch if there is trash to be picked up that didn't fit in the truck and notates the information in the file.

albi

CATEGORY 3

1. The Crew Chief performs the initial inspection of the property with the homeowner. The Crew Chief signs work authorization and performs a Matterport scan if the PM has not done so. The Crew Chief takes a full photo report.
2. The Crew Chief informs technicians of findings from the initial inspection and any PPE necessities or hazards in the area.
3. Set up damage containment barriers and install floor protection to cover and protect the floor leading to the affected area; self-adhesive plastic is laid over the paper. Note: When removing carpet, a roll of carpet is placed on the driveway to prevent dust from tracking outside. If not, then use rosin paper.
4. AFD is placed and runs on the job and during the mitigation and drying process.
5. Pour PRS on surface water greater than ½". Install submersible trash pumps if surface water exceeds ½". If not, skip this step.
6. Dehumidifiers are placed on the job and begin running.
7. Extract the water from the affected areas. Use a hard surface wand for hard surfaces and a carpet wand for the carpet. The extractor is hooked up to a garden hose and pumped into a toilet, or outside. Only Cat 1 and Cat 2 water may be pumped outside.
8. Material is removed from affected areas, covered and protected, and cleaned.
9. Remove the carpet and pad.
10. Remove Tiles (vinyl or ceramic) unless it's on a concrete substrate.
11. Remove Hardwood Flooring
12. Remove Laminate/ Engineered wood flooring and underlayment.
13. Interior walls: Remove baseboards and perform flood cuts.
14. Exterior walls: Perform flood cuts.
15. Remove Cabinetry/Vanities
16. Remove Ceilings
17. Remove Plaster
18. Once you remove affected materials, do a thorough cleaning and remove unnecessary floor protection. Conduct a low-pressure flush underneath sill plates. If possible, power wash the structure.
19. Antimicrobial is applied heavily to affected areas and deep cleaning with general cleaner. Once this is complete, hepa vacuuming takes place.
20. Drying equipment is placed per IICRC regulations. (1 air mover per every

albi

room, 1 AM per every 50-75 sqft of floor space and up to 2' high on walls, 1 air mover for every 150 sqft of the ceiling and wall space above 2' high, 1 air mover per each offset greater than 18". CF of air is divided by 50 to achieve the AHAM pints needed for dehu. Large DHM 135 AHAM regular size Dehu 70 AHAM).

21. After the work is complete, (the post mitigation Matterport Scan is complete) Crew Chiefs remove any unnecessary protection. They also conduct a final walk through with the clients, explaining their work in detail..
22. The Crew Chief sets up a date for equipment to be picked up with the client and calls dispatch to notify the date set. The Crew Chief asks dispatch if there is trash to be picked up that didn't fit in the truck and notates the information in the file.

If the Crew Chief runs into any issues with the project, they must notify their PM.

If the Crew Chief runs into any suspects for lead or asbestos, they must isolate the area and notify the PM. The project will continue to stabilize/ mitigate without disturbing said material.

If you're an Albi user, the job board is updated accordingly to reflect this information.

Equipment Pick Up

The office administrator contacts the client within 24 hours of starting the drying process. The purpose of the follow-up call is to confirm the pickup time and see if any other services are needed (i.e., reconstruction) and refer the project to that department. Check in to see if the client is satisfied with services thus far and answer any other questions the client may have. Any issues are referred back to the PM.

Dispatcher dispatches the Crew Chief for equipment pickup at the scheduled pickup time.

Crew verifies that the project has achieved dry standards, documents via photos, performs final cleaning, removes equipment, and does a final walk-through with the client. If the project is not yet dry, leave any necessary equipment on site, schedule another pickup date with the client and dispatch, and notify the PM of any issues or concerns the client may have.

A certificate of completion is signed, and notes are input into Albi. Make sure to ask the client to leave a review mentioning the crew's name, and if the client gives a positive review, provide them with a review rebate card. If it's self-pay, the Crew Chief collects the remaining balance.

If you're an Albi user, the job board and Albi are updated accordingly.

Invoicing

This should happen within 3-5 business days of equipment pick up ESRV Estimator reviews the project file and compiles an Xactimate estimate. The Estimator submits an email to the insurance carrier and billing with a signed work authorization, photo report, Xactimate Estimate, and Certificate of Completion.

The Accounts Receivable Specialist creates an invoice and replies to that email.

If you're an Albi user, the job board and AR Board are updated accordingly in Albi.

Accounts Receivable

It's the responsibility of the AR specialists to follow up with insurance companies and ensure that payments are made. If a dispute is made less than 10%, an AR specialist can waive it within reason. Any dispute greater than 10% will be referred to the Estimator and/or the ESRV Department. The Estimator has to coordinate with PMs if discrepancies exist.

AR specialists must follow up until the account is fully paid. The AR specialist must coordinate with dispatchers to collect payment if a check needs to be picked up from the client.

Intent to place lien is tendered to the client within 60 days by the Administrative Manager.

An Administrative Manager places a lien when payment is not received within 90 days and notifies the General Manager.

The job board and Albi are updated accordingly.

File Close

An Administrative Department manager reviews the file before its final completion and closure. |File Closing Process|

The job board and Albi are updated accordingly.

THE 4 PILLARS:
Wealth, Health, Love, and Spirituality

In the second half of 2021, I was at the top of my game. Albi was going great, my wife was several months pregnant with our daughter, and I had been traveling, speaking at different conferences for Albi. I had my family, I had wealth, I had my new company–everything was looking up, except one area: my physical health. (I guess in some ways, it was looking "up," too—my weight was up over 200 pounds!)

I didn't worry too much about my weight—I was doing well financially, so a little extra weight couldn't hurt, right? Well, suddenly, in the midst of all that, I got COVID, and then, my lack of attention to my health took a very, very, dramatic toll on my life.

I was only in my late twenties, but after two weeks of typical COVID symptoms, my oxygen levels began to drop to life-threatening levels; I ended up with multiple hospital visits in a span of two weeks. Towards the end, my oxygen dropped so low, I needed thirteen liters of oxygen just to maintain my blood-oxygen levels. As I lay trapped in the hospital for the second time in my life (I'll get to that in a bit), needing four to five times the amount of oxygen most people need, I realized my physical health was essential—by not taking care of this one area of my life, I could have lost everything—my wife, my baby, my family, my business, my wealth.

While I survived, my weight contributed to multiple complications—I ended up with blood clots for four months, and had "long COVID" symptoms. So, instead of recovering in a matter of weeks as most young people would have, it took me nearly a year. Now, we don't know *exactly* how much my physical condition contributed, but we know with almost total certainty, that if I had been healthier before COVID, I would have recovered much quicker and easier.

This experience taught me that despite having everything else in the world going for me, without my health, all that I loved became threatened.

Throughout my life, I'd had different experiences that taught me about the pillars of what makes up an important life—I'd also believed in the power of money. That came instinctually to me as an immigrant who grew up with widely varying amounts of it. But love? I had to learn about that the hard way. Spirituality? Another learning lesson. Then, COVID taught me the final pillar of what I call the "4 Pillars of Life": wealth, health, love, and spirituality. Others have used these four pillars, or similar ones, to describe the most important elements of life. My friend Dan has seven, technically. Some talk about the "4 Fs": Faith, Family, Fitness, and finances.

My pillars aren't so far off those, and I keep them top of mind so I never got caught up with only one of them, and thereby trick myself into thinking I'm "Making" it, when, in reality, I'm just choosing one over the other.

These are the pillars of a good life, one that's solid, that can't be shaken, and when you have all of them, whatever else happens on top of the foundation, won't affect these. But, if you crack a central pillar in the foundation, everything else can come crumbling down. Here's how to build a solid foundation from the ground up:

Wealth

Coming from a first-generation immigrant household, my central focus growing up was money. At the time, I didn't understand the difference between riches and wealth. Money was money. It allowed me to buy what I wanted to buy and go where I wanted to go. At the age of twenty-one, I had a net worth in the millions, but I learned after that *wealth* and *riches* are not quite the same.

Wealth implies assets that can create income over time. In other words, having a business, property, investments, etc., that continue to build and generate income for those I love. I *was* fairly rich by the time I was twenty-one, but *wealthy?* Not quite. I still had a lot to learn.

Health

I told you about my COVID scare in 2021. Since then, I've been on a trajectory to improving my physical health. I didn't change everything overnight. Rather, I started working out, eating healthier, and instituting real, life-changing long-term habits that have impacted me for the better.

By now, I'm under 200 pounds, and I've even done the 75 Hard challenge, and I'm feeling great.

Love

I've had two near-death experiences. I already described the recent one, that had to do with COVID. But there was another—In August 2016, I overdosed. It was a stupid decision, one I instantly regretted, but it changed the course of my life, eventually, for the better. By then, I'd given up *everything* in pursuit of money, and I'd let my relationships fall to the wayside. Luckily, my family cared so much about me, that even after my ignorance of them, they showed up at the hospital and showed up in my life to show me what real love is.

From that day on, I approached the business through a new perspective. I no longer let myself work to the point of exhaustion, sacrificing time with my girlfriend (now wife), to see the business flourish by my own hand.

Spirituality

In all honesty, I'm still figuring this one out, but one thing has "haunted" me, in the best way:

The night that I ended up in the hospital needing thirteen liters of oxygen to keep my blood-oxygen levels up, a miracle happened. You see, I'd shown up to the hospital several times, only to be told to go away, that I was "young and relatively healthy," and didn't need oxygen. But that night, something told me to go anyway. I showed up, expecting to hear the same song and dance. But while I was there, at the hospital, my oxygen suddenly dropped *dangerously* low.

If I hadn't decided to come to the hospital when I did, I would have been asleep in my bed when that sudden drop occurred... and I'm not sure I'd be here today.

I don't know everything there is to know about spirituality, but I now there's someone out there who wants me here, and I believe that's true for you, too.

You're not an accident, or a mistake. You have some purpose to this grand life, and despite yesterday, there's a tomorrow.

Let's go grab it.

ABOUT THE AUTHOR:

In 2014, Alex Duta and his father co-founded Romexterra, a fire and water damage restoration company based out of Chicago, Illinois. As they scaled their own restoration business, Alex recognized the lack of technology solutions built for the restoration industry. So, in 2020, after growing Romexterra to eight figures, Alex co-founded Albi—a software company with the first platform built exclusively for restorers and others in the trades. Albi officially joined Y Combinator in 2022, where they gained interest from a variety of venture capitalists. Albi, their flagship product, went live in 2021, and it's quickly become the restoration industry's leading technology solution. In addition to running Albi as the CEO, Alex coaches restorers across North America, and is also a keynote speaker at conferences, such as Albi's *Evolve* conference for restorers, launched in 2024.

ABOUT THE AUTHOR

Made in United States
Orlando, FL
15 May 2024

46913772R00157